TOUCH OF LOVE

Paramhansa Yogananda

TOUCH OF LOVE

LIVING THE TEACHINGS OF
Paramhansa Yogananda

NAYASWAMIS JYOTISH and DEVI

Crystal Clarity Publishers,
Los Angeles, California
Copyright 2020 by Hansa Trust
All rights reserved.

Crystal Clarity Publishers
Los Angeles, CA
800 424 1055

clarity@crystalclarity.com
www.crystalclarity.com

© 2020 by Hansa Trust. All rights reserved.

CONTENTS

Preface | *ix*
1. Searching for Gold | *1*
2. The Love of the Guru | *4*
3. The Power of Zero Resistance | *6*
4. Saved by the Guru | *8*
5. Balancing the Scales | *10*
6. Dry Spells | *12*
7. God Goes on Vacation | *14*
8. "You Have No Idea How Beautiful You Are" | *16*
9. The Sacred Hidden River | *18*
10. My India | *21*
11. Seeing the Possibilities | *24*
12. Four Keys to Deeper Meditations | *26*
13. Who Are You? Truth vs. Facts | *29*
14. Is Happiness a Choice? | *31*
15. Look to the Mountaintop | *34*
16. Fifty Years | *37*
17. The Nature of Divine Love | *39*
18. Global Warming | *41*
19. Life, Liberty, and the Pursuit of Happiness | *44*
20. Godly Qualities — A Checklist | *46*
21. Meditation — Is It Hard or Easy? | *49*
22. A Virtual Universe? | *52*
23. The Best Way to Deal with Change | *54*
24. Unity in Diversity | *56*
25. The Solution Lies Within the Problem | *58*
26. Unifying Principles | *61*

27. The Strength Remains | *63*
28. The Channel Is Blessed | *65*
29. The Art of Becoming | *67*
30. Focus | *69*
31. Lessons from a Dance Class | *72*
32. The Challenges of Life | *75*
33. Does Satan Exist? | *78*
34. The Eclipse | *80*
35. How to Control Desires | *82*
36. Becoming a Guardian Angel | *84*
37. The Secret of a Remarkable Life | *87*
38. The Crucible | *90*
39. The Sparrow, Each Grain of Sand | *92*
40. Feeding the Ants | *95*
41. Who's In Charge Here? | *97*
42. The Darkest Night of the Year | *99*
43. Your Brain on Meditation | *101*
44. Seclusion | *103*
45. The Broken Shell | *106*
46. The Mouse Family | *109*
47. What We Saw | *111*
48. Babaji's Advice | *114*
49. Is It Possible to Stop Worrying? | *116*
50. God, Gurus, Gurubhais, and Grit | *119*
51. The Shawl of Gold | *121*
52. Resolutions | *123*
53. Finding Your Own Spiritual Power in 2018 | *126*
54. Teamwork | *128*
55. Touching the Silence | *131*
56. Ananda Seva | *134*
57. When to Fight Back | *137*
58. We Need New Self-Definitions | *140*
59. The Happiness Thieves | *143*
60. The Pillars of the Path | *146*
61. "The Art of Following": An Allegory | *148*

62. Amazing Day, Amazing Grace | *151*
63. What Is This Life? | *154*
64. A Place of Refuge | *156*
65. Whom Are You Trying to Please? | *158*
66. Cooperating with Grace | *161*
67. Express Your Self! | *163*
68. The Power of Divine Places | *166*
69. Beauty and Grace | *168*
70. Self-Control | *170*
71. Five Steps to Self-Realization | *173*
72. We Don't Know Enough | *176*
73. The Philosopher King | *179*
74. Game Over | *181*
75. How to Water a Garden | *183*
76. Animals and Compassion | *186*
77. A Day of Yoga | *188*
78. Acting on Intuition | *191*
79. Everything Balances Out in the End | *194*
80. The Most Important Thing I Do | *196*
81. Leaving the Morgue | *198*
82. What Should I Do? | *201*
83. We Are Building a Temple of Light | *204*
84. Tools for Living | *206*
85. How to Build Inner Power | *209*
86. Living a Life of Discipleship | *212*
87. God's Boatman | *214*
88. From Nowhere to Now Here | *217*
89. What's Left? | *220*
90. Keeping It Simple | *223*
91. The Well, the Bucket, and the Rope | *225*
92. An Exultation of Music | *227*
93. Integrity vs. Showmanship | *230*
94. The Power of a Positive Mind | *232*
95. Quit Counting! | *235*
96. Five Quick Stress Breakers | *238*

97. Just Do It | *241*
98. How to Make Better Decisions | *244*
99. Lessons Learned | *247*
100. Sing Your Way to Freedom | *250*
101. Thank You, Dear India | *253*
102. Son-Bathing | *256*
103. Who Is the Other Wise Man? | *258*
104. My New Year's Resolutions | *262*
    Photographers and Artists | *267*
    About the Authors | *270*

PREFACE

When we began writing our weekly blog, "A Touch of Light," in 2013, we had no idea if we would really have something meaningful to say every week, or if people would enjoy reading them. And so we were gratified when both of these questions were answered with a resounding "YES!"

Each week some unexpected insight or inspiration would come, and one of us would say to the other, "I think this would make a good blog." (We take turns writing them, so we each have an intervening week to draw ideas.) As the weeks passed, we began to realize that the source of our inspirations was not our own, but that we were being inwardly guided to write what would be spiritually helpful to the readers. In many cases it was that simple: What inspired us also inspired others.

Then the comments and "likes" started coming in from people around the world telling us how much support and help they were getting from the blogs. One comment that comes in almost every week is, "This arrived at just the moment I needed to read it. Thank you."

Many readers also tell us that they look forward every Friday morning (when the blog is posted) to see what inspiration lies in store for them. A number have said that they keep one of the books by their bedside, so they can read something short and uplifting before sleep.

So here we are, six years and more than three hundred blogs later, and we're still writing them—and people are still reading. Our first book of those blogs, *Touch of Light*, covered the years 2013–2014. The next, *Touch of Joy*, was for 2015–2016. And now you hold in your hands the collection from 2017–2018, *Touch of Love*.

The books have been a wonderful evolution from "light" to "joy" and finally to "love." As we increasingly felt the enthusiasm and support of our readers, it no longer felt (as it sometimes did in the beginning) that we were writing in a vacuum. Over the years, we began to feel the warmth, gratitude, and friendship with which these blogs were being received, and writing them truly became an expression of love.

So we offer them now to you with our love, and with the hope that you find in these pages the guidance, inspiration, and insight that you are seeking.

With light, joy, and love,
NAYASWAMIS JYOTISH AND DEVI

1
Jan. 5, 2017

SEARCHING *for* GOLD

Historians tell us that medieval alchemists were continually in search of the elusive "philosophers' stone," that mythical substance which could turn base metals into gold. As far as we know, they never succeeded in their quest, but there is a different kind of philosophers' stone which we have already discovered.

The guru is that philosophers' stone, for he or she transmutes the base metal of our ego into the pure gold of God-realization. The guru's power, however, goes beyond even this. Swami Kriyananda once said that the guru's inner touch ultimately transforms us into his own likeness—giving us the ability, to a greater or lesser degree, to transform others. In other words, we, too, become a philosophers' stone.

In this new year, as we make resolutions to cast aside bad habits and adopt new ones for self-improvement, let's not limit ourselves to activities that are, in the last analysis, still tied to the post of ego. Let's also look at ways that we can unite our awareness with that of God and Guru. Here are some suggestions:

Try to see all circumstances in your life from the broadest, most impersonal perspective. When difficulties arise, don't think, "Oh, why is this happening to *me*?" Rather consider, "Something has happened of which I, and others, are a part." Try to feel that you are only a small component of a greater reality. Look for the one divine consciousness behind the seeming diversity of perspectives and events.

Meditate on and inwardly repeat these lines from Yogananda's poem "*Samadhi*":

> I, the Cosmic Sea,
> Watch the little ego floating in me.

See the full poem at *joyiswith.in/16*.

Judge no one, but accept all as expressions of God — as part of your own Self. Once when Swami Kriyananda was meditating in one of the sacred sites of Assisi, Italy, where St. Francis had lived, he was overwhelmed by a sense of inner sweetness. Feeling that this was the presence of St. Francis, Swamiji prayed to him, "How is such sweetness possible?" The answer that came to him in an instant was, "By never judging anyone, but accepting all as children of God." The good and evil in this world are also a part of each one of us, which we can transcend and help others as well to transcend.

Meditate on and repeat these words from "*Samadhi*":

> Anger, greed, good, bad, salvation, lust,
> I swallowed, transmuted all
> Into a vast ocean of blood of my own one Being!

In 2017 live with the strength of will, courage, and determination to be a channel for God's love and joy under all circumstances. Clutch the "philosophers' stone" of Guru's grace to your bosom, and pray that all the dross within you be melted away. Walk on inner paths that you haven't before trod. Develop the courage to cast aside the old you, and to allow the power of the guru to flow through you unimpeded.

Meditate on and repeat these words from Yogananda's poem, "The Noble New":

> Love all with love that none have felt, and brave
> The battle of life with strength unchained.

United with you in our inner quest,
NAYASWAMI DEVI

THE LOVE *of the* GURU

The love and friendship of the guru are something that is hard for us to understand, much less accept. We, who are limited in time and space, naturally relate to the guru in the same way. How often I've thought and heard others say, "If only I had been with Master." This thought, sweet though it is, actually ends up distancing us from him.

He *is* with us now as we read this. He said, "To those who *think* me near, I will be near." If we open ourselves to him, if we invite him into our life, he will become a dynamic presence in our lives.

We recently received this beautiful letter by Paramhansa Yogananda. It is deeply touching and reassuring. We shared it with our friends here at Ananda Village and now, dear friend, we offer it to you.

NAYASWAMI JYOTISH

"To those who think me near, I will be near."

A Letter from Master, November 1933

To my friends, in all lands and in all worlds, greetings and good will! Wherever you are, whoever you are, of whatever color, race, or creed, I send you my love and the pledge of my loyalty. You, who for thousands of years, or for only a day, have worked and fought for justice, freedom, and Truth, receive my gratitude and devotion.

You who dwell in palaces or hovels, in cities or jungles, in mansions or dungeons — if in your hearts there is the urge toward higher, better living and loftier ideals, believe me when I say I am your friend and that I count you blessed friends of mine.

Many of you I have known in the past, and some of you I have never seen, but I think that in God's appointed time I shall meet each one of you face to face and give you proof of my affection. However, it matters little that we are not together now, nor does it matter that time and space may separate us by almost infinite distances. The only thing that counts is that we are friends, working together in a common cause, the cause of righteousness and the expansion of the consciousness of the children of the Most High.

Although I see you not, I often feel your presence near, or thrill with the noble thoughts which you send out to find their home in minds attuned to yours. Although you may never read the words which I am penning now, I declare to you that you shall feel the vibrations of tenderness and kindliness which emanate from me to all of you.

Our work, our love, our purposes are One. March on, dear friends, to higher, brighter goals! Continue in your dreams of happier days and in your deeds of service to your kind. Protect the torch of faith from winds of doubt, and let no storm disturb your peace of mind. Farewell, dear friends of mine, until we meet.

— PARAMHANSA YOGANANDA —
East-West magazine, November 1933

3
Jan. 19, 2017

The POWER *of* ZERO RESISTANCE

Once Paramhansa Yogananda was attending a wedding with some of his disciples, and at a certain point he began handing out different-colored roses to the women devotees. After receiving her rose from the Guru, one woman expressed disappointedly, "But I wanted a pink rose, not a red one."

Yogananda looked at her, and with unexpected intensity replied, "What *I* give, *you* take."

The human tendency to want to change the circumstances of our life to accord more closely with our desires is a deeply ingrained aspect of the ego. The Master was teaching the disciple the importance not only of accepting impartially whatever comes to us, but also of being totally open to God's taking charge. Having little or no resistance to God's will allows us to move beyond the bondage of likes and dislikes towards inner freedom.

In contrast to this story, we recently heard a remarkable tale about Anandamayee Ma, one of India's great women saints who passed away in the early 1980s. In one of her ashrams there lives today a joyful, radiant monk who recently shared with some of the Ananda monks about his life.

When this monk was a little boy of about six years old, his mother, a devotee of Anandamayee Ma, brought him to Ma for her blessing. As Ma reached out her hand to bless him she paused, and then, looking directly into his mother's eyes, asked, "Will you give me your son?" The mother nodded, and Ma invited the lad to come forward and sit close to her. And that was the beginning of his life in God.

Now a grown man, the monk shared that he never felt any separation from family: at one point he was cared for by one mother, and then by another, but he always felt surrounded by love.

What is the spiritual lesson this story demonstrates? *What God asks, we give.* Judged from the point of view of a traditional family, this incident may seem unsettling. But considered from the perspective of someone seeking freedom from ego attachments, it shows the power and blessing of overcoming all resistance to God's will.

For years scientists have worked with something called "superconductors": various materials that, when cooled to very low temperatures, conduct electricity with absolutely no resistance on an atomic level. Because of this, electrical current can flow perfectly through the conduit, and great magnetic power can be generated.

We, too, can become "superconscious superconductors" when we:

1. Cool down and stop struggling against God's will,
2. Remove the resistances of the ego, and
3. Allow the power of divine current to flow through us unimpeded.

As the words in one of Master's chants say, "Then joy is sweet, sorrow a dream, when Thy song flows through me, Lord."

In divine friendship,
NAYASWAMI DEVI

Swami Kriyananda in the Lahiri Mandir at Ananda Village.

4
Jan. 26, 2017

SAVED *by the* GURU

A dear friend, Nayaswami Devarshi, is a longtime Ananda member who is now serving in India as the head of our Monastic Order. He sent this letter to us last week.

"A very miraculous save by the Guru here at Mumbai airport, on our way to Singapore. As Aditya [a fellow monk] and I were standing in line to leave the country, I realized I didn't have an additional document that I needed in order to show residency in India, which is required for me to be able to leave and return, because of the type of visa I have.

"As Aditya [a native speaker] said later, one of the immigration officials said to the other, 'Take a careful look at these two. They are disciples of Yogananda.' He had been at your recent talk in Mumbai, and he recognized Aditya and me!!! He's still reading *Autobiography of a Yogi* and other books, and preparing to take classes in Mumbai.

"To remember us, in our civilian clothes, and that we ran into him in a city of 20 million . . . even then, I was barely allowed through. Will try to get a scanned copy for the return."

Divine Mother and the Guru are constantly looking out for us. A few years ago, I had a reading from a book of ancient prophecies. The pundit giving the reading told me, "The Guru is watching over you moment by moment and second by second." This is true for all his sincere disciples.

It is thrilling to have his protection demonstrated in a "miraculous save." Knowing Devarshi as I do, I am sure that afterward he expressed his gratitude mentally in this manner: "Thank you, Divine Mother and Master, for your protection and your grace. I will do my best to learn from this experience."

But if we are grateful for only the pleasant things, we are missing the point. We must be grateful for *everything*. One time someone said to Swami Kriyananda, referring to one of his many illnesses, "It doesn't seem fair of Divine Mother." Swamiji corrected her, immediately and strongly: "I am grateful for whatever Divine Mother gives me. I know that everything that comes is an expression of Her love."

So, what if Devarshi had been sent back? What if that official had said something like, "You are a disciple of Yogananda and should not be so careless as to have forgotten your papers. I'm sure he wants me to teach you a lesson!"?

If that had happened, what should Devarshi's prayer have been? Knowing him, I suspect that it would have been the same: "Thank you, Divine Mother and Master, for your protection and your grace. I will do my best to learn from this experience."

Everything that comes to us, the pleasant and unpleasant, is an expression of divine love and protection. Unwavering gratitude is how we become aware of God's constant blessings and protection.

Here is an affirmation that I wrote many years ago and still often repeat:

> I am grateful for my life,
>   exactly as it is.
> I am thankful for this day.
> I welcome every hour.
> Thank you, God. Thank
>   you, God.

In gratitude,
NAYASWAMI JYOTISH

"A Perfect Day," by Nayaswami Jyotish.

5
Feb. 2, 2017

BALANCING *the* SCALES

Dr. Shinichi Suzuki, founder of the world-renowned Suzuki School of Music Education, was a humanitarian as well as a pioneer in musical training for children. In his book, *Nurtured by Love*, Dr. Suzuki shares a story that has relevance for us today.

He, his wife, and their two small children were living in Matsumoto, Japan in the painful, chaotic period following the end of World War II. Dr. Suzuki was a violinist and music teacher, and though Japan was in a state of economic and social upheaval, his family was able to maintain a simple, refined way of life.

Learning that one of his prewar students was now a homeless war orphan, Dr. Suzuki and his wife brought this young boy into their home. After some weeks of trying to work with him, Mrs. Suzuki felt that the situation was hopeless and said to her husband, "I am sorry, but I cannot handle this boy—he has no manners and no sense of obedience. He is disrupting the harmony of our home."

Dr. Suzuki replied, "You are right. He has lost all discipline and refinement, so *we* must all be even more disciplined in *our* behavior." Eventually, surrounded by love and courtesy, the little orphan assimilated the vibrations of the Suzuki home and became an integral part of the family.

What can we learn from this story? We, too, are living in chaotic times, in which truth, compassion, and selflessness are being superseded by lies, callousness, self-interest, and greed.

Swami Kriyananda once said, "Ananda's mission is to help equalize the world on the spiritual plane." This is true not only for

Ananda, but for all people who wish to see the spirit of universal love and unity prevail. In order to counter those values we reject, we need to try even harder to express those that we cherish.

Here are some suggestions for balancing the scales of negativity to effect positive changes around us:

Balance Fear with Inner Peace. If you haven't yet started a daily practice of meditation, begin today. If you are already a regular meditator, challenge yourself each day to continue your practice until you feel God's unshakable peace within. Then share that peace with others.

Balance Negativity Towards People with Acceptance and Compassion. Watch your inner reactions throughout the day. If you find yourself judging others, or viewing them critically, counter this by consciously expressing kindness in thought and deed. Love is the greatest power in the universe, and in its presence darkness cannot remain.

Balance Selfishness and Greed with a Spirit of Generosity and Service. Look for ways that you can give more of yourself and help those less fortunate. Offer to serve others selflessly without any thought of reward. This will help to balance the vibrations of self-interest that are so prevalent now.

Balance Comes from Living at Your Own Center. Swami Kriyananda wrote: "Live as much as possible at the midpoint between all opposites: That is where the Infinite Spirit dwells. Everything in Creation is dual. Every 'up' is canceled by a 'down'; light is balanced by darkness; pleasure, by pain. Eternal truths lie at the point midway between all opposites. Therefore I say, live more at your center, in the heart."

Joined with you in the One Self,

NAYASWAMI DEVI

Ananda's mission is to help equalize the world on the spiritual plane.

6
Feb. 9, 2017

DRY SPELLS

It is a little ironic for me to be writing about this subject just now. Here at Ananda Village, in Northern California, we're in the midst of yet another major storm, experiencing the greatest rainfall in over twenty years. The rivers are roaring, the reservoirs are full, the mountain snowpack is huge, and more is on the way. Maybe, just maybe, getting soaked whenever I step outside is what got me thinking about dry spells. But let's move on from the weather and talk about those spiritual dry spells and how to deal with them.

What triggers a spiritual drought? Here are three important causes: lack of will power, a temporary drop in our "specific gravity," and the effects of past karma. The way to deal with each of them is different.

Photo of the Yuba River by Barbara Bingham.

Lack of will power. Paramhansa Yogananda defined will as "desire plus energy directed toward a goal," and said that every test is a test of will. We might think that the solution to a dry spell of this nature would be to put out more effort. Generally speaking, this is wrong. Will power, it turns out, functions somewhat like a muscle. It gets fatigued by overuse and too much stress. It is stronger in the morning, when we are fresh, and wanes throughout the day and during the week. If you want someone to grant your request, try to ask him on a Monday morning.

Athletes know that overtraining leads to injury. We spiritual athletes, too, can push hard when we are fresh, but need consciously to relax when we're tired. For me, this means that my morning meditations are longer, deeper, more focused on techniques, and more intense. I have more will power when I'm feeling rested. In the evenings, I tend to do more inward chanting and adopt a "softer" approach to my sadhana. But everyone is different, so work with your own rhythms. Self-discipline is absolutely necessary, but should be applied with discrimination.

Specific gravity is how light or heavy our consciousness is, how sattwic or tamasic. If your specific gravity is lower than usual, then be more careful to avoid people, places, entertainment, and even foods that pull you down. As with will power, our specific gravity tends to drop when we're tired. Build in rest periods, do things that are fun and uplifting, monitor your energy level, and you'll find that you will quickly pop back up to your normal buoyancy. Then you can try to go even higher.

The effects of past karma. Spiritual dry spells are generally due to past moods, indulgences, and lack of discipline. Counteract their effects by making the right spiritual effort now. What is the *right* effort? In the Bhagavad Gita Krishna says, "Yoga is not for him who eats too much or who fasts too much, who sleeps too much or who sleeps too little."

In other words, efforts that are balanced and consistent gradually overcome internal resistance. When our energy flows without resistance, we find that we have plenty of will power and a buoyant specific gravity, and that past karma loses its force.

Finally, pray for God and Guru to help you in your efforts. Remember, they are on your side.

In joyful balance,
NAYASWAMI JYOTISH

7

Feb. 16, 2017

GOD GOES *on* VACATION

Aloha! We're currently relaxing on Kauai, one of the beautiful Hawaiian Islands, on a two-week vacation that was gifted to us by many friends from Ananda. One hears "Aloha" everywhere here, because it's a word with multiple meanings: "hello," "good-bye," "love," "compassion," and "welcome."

It's considered one of the most sacred and powerful of all Hawaiian words, having the literal meaning "together in the breath of God." This greeting is reminiscent of the common Indian one, "Namaste," which means, "My soul bows to your soul."

We had a wonderful experience of God's constant protection after landing in the airport in Kauai. Assuming that we could easily rent a car after arriving, we'd neglected to reserve one in advance. As we waited for the shuttle buses from the different car rental agencies to come pick up passengers, we noticed that everyone but us already had vouchers in their hands.

As the buses pulled up, we asked four successive drivers if they had any cars available for people without reservations. Invariably they replied, "No, everything is already taken." Starting to feel a little desperate, we put our question once again to the next bus driver who arrived.

Hanalei Bay, Kauai. Painting "Hanalei Bay" by Nayaswami Jyotish.

After putting in a call to his office, he told us there was a chance, and we boarded his bus.

We arrived at their office to a line of about twenty people ahead of us — all with reservations. The thought kept running through our minds, "How will we get to our rental unit across the island without a car?"

After a thirty-minute wait it was finally our turn, and a bright, energetic woman asked our name. Before we could tell her we didn't have a reservation, she began typing into her computer, then looked up and said, "We don't have any record of your reservation. Maybe you didn't complete it properly. How long are you planning to stay?"

"Two weeks," we answered, a little sheepishly.

She smiled, and in the true "aloha spirit," replied, "Let's see what we can do." After making several phone calls, she looked up, smiled, and announced, "We've got a car for you, and I'm going to give it to you at the best possible rate."

We shook our heads in amazement at the goodness of people, and at God's ever-watchful eye. The incident reminded us of the time Swami Kriyananda decided at the last minute to go on a vacation to Carmel, California, to celebrate his completion of *The Art and Science of Raja Yoga*.

It was the height of the tourist season, and having made no hotel reservation he found only one room available, at a price he wasn't sure he could afford. As he registered, Swamiji took out his wallet to pay in advance, lest he not have enough money at the end of his stay to cover the cost. The clerk said, "No, don't pay me. I'll put you down as a travel agent and give you a free stay."

I guess God likes to go on vacations sometimes, too. In any case, whether or not He shows Himself so openly, we should remember that His love, which underlies everything, is always with us.

In the spirit of Aloha,
NAYASWAMI DEVI

Feb. 23, 2017

"YOU HAVE NO IDEA HOW BEAUTIFUL YOU ARE"

I am writing this from the Island of Kauai, the northernmost island of the Hawaiian chain. It's certainly one of the most beautiful places on earth, set like a gemstone in an aqua sea. Its hills, valleys, swaying plants, and even its people have been shaped by centuries of rain, sun, and wind. It's as if Divine Mother had said to Herself, "Here I will put on My loveliest attire. I will wear a hundred subtle shades of green, and My jewelry will be brilliant flowers and birds of every color. In the evenings, I will turn My clouds luminescent and color them orange, and red, and lavender. And I will surround Myself with crystalline blue waters, and even these I will fill with the most fantastic fish I can imagine."

"Bee Balm." Photograph by Craig P. Burrows.

And yet, no matter how perfect the scenery seems, it is the least of Her wonders. We saw some remarkable photos taken by Craig P. Burrows (they can be seen on his website: cpburrows.com) using a process by which ultraviolet light causes a flower to fluoresce, or emit its own light. Beyond the visible spectrum, in a world revealed by infrared, ultraviolet, x-rays, and other means, is a world of amazing beauty that cannot be seen with our eyes.

People who have highly developed intuition can perceive the realms that lie beyond the senses. Paramhansa Yogananda once told a group of disciples, "You have no idea how beautiful you are. I see you all as beings of light." His consciousness was altogether beyond the limitations of this physical dream world. He knew that the physical plane, no matter how lovely, was only the dimmest reflection of what awaits us.

Yogananda came into this world in order to show us how to overcome our limitations and experience the true beauty of our higher Self. The whole universe is really consciousness, not matter, and the spiritual practices he taught are meant to detach us from the ego's delusion that this material plane is the ultimate reality. To find the beauty that lies both within and without, we must calm the mind, the emotions, and ultimately the breath.

Yogananda wrote, "Come out of your closed chamber of limitation. Breathe in the fresh air of vital thoughts. Exhale poisonous thoughts of discouragement, discontentment, or hopelessness. Never suggest to your mind human limitations of sickness, old age, or death, but constantly remind yourself, 'I am the Infinite, which has become the body.'"

It is not that we should ignore the incredible loveliness of this world. After all, God made it for us to enjoy. But, in our enjoyment, we should try to see beneath the surface. When we allow Divine Mother to show us Her true self, everything becomes filled with light and beauty.

In the light,
NAYASWAMI JYOTISH

9
March 2, 2017

The SACRED HIDDEN RIVER

While in Hawaii, I read a translation of an ancient Hawaiian song about *mana*, or "life force":

> For mana is divine power
> And we Hawaiians have a keen awareness of this
>   Supernatural force running through all things.
> For it is our natural consciousness to be psychic.
>   And we read signs and omens into elemental
>   phenomena.
> To us, there is nothing that isn't alive.
> For everything has mana in some form . . .
> Rocks and plants and mountains, winds and sea.
> And water in all its forms is the symbol for this
>   Mystical power called mana.

As I read this, I was struck by the similarity of *mana* to the yogic concept of *prana*. The techniques that Paramhansa Yogananda taught—his Energization Exercises and several techniques of meditation, most especially Kriya Yoga—are expressly designed to heighten our awareness of this subtle life force around and within us.

Yoganandaji wrote, "I watch the roaring, shouting torrent of life-force moving through the heart into the body. I turn backward to the spine. The beat and roar of the heart are gone. Like a sacred

Paramhansa Yogananda on the Ganges.

hidden river my life-force flows in the gorge of the spine. I enter a dim corridor through the door of the spiritual eye, and speed on until at last the river of my life flows into the ocean of Life and loses itself in bliss."

It isn't only through the practice of techniques that the flow of prana can be experienced. To enhance our awareness of it, right attitude, also, is vitally important. Positive thinking and enthusiasm open the floodgates of our mind to an increased flow of energy. And a spirit of respect towards all people unites us with the great river of life.

There is a remarkable story that I read in a book about the ancient Hawaiian civilization. A Christian missionary came to the South Pacific in the late 1800s with a burning zeal to convert the "heathen." One of his methods of "persuasion" was to condemn the traditional priests as charlatans and fakers.

One day after a particularly vehement tirade against the ancient ways, an elderly priest asked the missionary why he always attacked them when he had no knowledge of their true spiritual power.

"Because you are liars," the missionary said defiantly. "If you have such great powers, why don't you demonstrate them now for all the people to see?"

Thus mercilessly taunted by the missionary, the old priest finally shook his head slowly, and, in a quiet voice, said, "Go down this pathway into the jungle about one hundred yards. There you will find a fork in the road. Take the right-hand fork, proceed a few more steps, then stop and look into the jungle."

With the whole congregation watching, the missionary did as he'd been instructed and looked into the jungle. What he saw appeared to be an open window displaying a scene from another time and place. Through the window he saw his mother's kitchen in Holland, where she stood—just as he often remembered her since leaving the family home—baking bread. Glancing up, she looked directly at her son, who fled screaming in fear of the extraordinary power that had been demonstrated to him.

This experience so changed him that he left the village, abandoned his missionary work, and spent the rest of his life studying the ways of the traditional religion. He later received a letter from his mother asking if he was well, because she also had seen him that day, and was concerned that perhaps what she'd seen was his ghost.

To feel the river of life within us, we need to see the Divine Life in all. As Swami Kriyananda wrote in his song, "Brothers": "Though words and customs vary like waves upon the sea / One life beneath the surface binds everyone to me."

United with you in spirit,
NAYASWAMI DEVI

10
March 7, 2017

MY INDIA

As I write these words it's March 7, the 65th anniversary of Paramhansa Yogananda's *mahasamadhi* (conscious exit from the body). He left this earth in a dramatic fashion. At a banquet in Los Angeles in honor of the visiting Indian ambassador, after a short and very sweet talk, the great master recited his poem, "My India." As he read the final lines, his body slipped to the floor, and his soul departed for higher realms. He had predicted the time of his passing and had said that he wanted to die "with his boots on" serving, as he always had, as a teacher and model to all receptive seekers.

A great master's acts are never without intention, especially such a significant one. Let us look at "My India," not as just a lovely poem, but as his final words of advice to us. The last touching sentences are:

> Hail, Thou mother of religions, lotus, scenic beauties,
>   and great sages!
> Thy doors are open wide to welcome
> God's true sons from every corner of the earth,
> Where Ganges, woods, Himalayan caves, and men
>   dream God.
> I am hallowed; my body touched that sod!

The essence of the poem is the essence of his entire mission: The Purpose of Life is to Know God. The poem begins:

Not where the musk of happiness blows,
Not in lands where darkness and fears never tread,
Not in homes where unceasing smiles reign,
Nor in Heaven nor prosperous lands
Would I be born.
If once more I must assume a mortal garb,
A thousand famines may wrack my body,
Waste my flesh, and leave me prostrate,
Yet would I be born again in Hindustan.
  A million thieves of disease
May steal my flesh,
And clouds of fate
Send scalding showers of searing sorrow—
Yet would I prefer in India to reappear!
. . .
Because it was there I first learned
To love God, and all things beautiful.

What happens to us, what conditions we must face, what trials we must overcome are not important. What is essential is that we make the search for God the focus of our lives. Swami Kriyananda often said, "The great masters don't come in order to clean up our mud puddles. They come to help us get out of them." In his poem Yogananda says that, if I must dream another birth, let me not seek a pleasant one, but rather let my dream be filled with yearning to know God.

Photo by *Nayaswami Jyotish*. "*It felt like a blessing from Master,*" he said of this "*cloud rainbow,*" which was unlike any he'd ever seen before. It appeared outside his living room window on the day he wrote this blog, the anniversary of *Yogananda's* mahasamadhi.

Birth and rebirth may seem far off, but each evening's sleep is like a little death, as we shed awareness of this body and ego. And each morning is a little rebirth, as we awake yet again from the forgotten worlds of slumber. Before we sleep, let us resolve to be reborn in the morning in the state of consciousness where God is foremost. And when we awaken in the morning, let our first thought be, "Let this day, above all else, be dedicated 'to love God, and all things beautiful.'"

Paramhansa Yogananda begins *Autobiography of a Yogi*, his spiritual classic, with these words: "The characteristic features of Indian culture have long been a search for ultimate verities and the concomitant disciple-guru relationship." This, above all else, is India's gift to the world. If we live in that consciousness, we, too, can say at the end of life, "I am hallowed; my body touched that sod!"

In deepest appreciation,
NAYASWAMI JYOTISH

11
March 16, 2017

SEEING *the* POSSIBILITIES

There is a story about two shoe salesmen who are sent by their companies to explore the possibilities for sales in a Third-World country. They arrive at the same time, check out the scene, and then both head for the telegraph office to report back.

The first one wires: "Everyone barefoot here. No market. Returning immediately."

The second one writes, "No one has shoes here. Tremendous opportunities. Send large shipment immediately." He saw the possibilities.

When Paramhansa Yogananda arrived in America in 1920, he hadn't a friend in the world and only five hundred dollars to his name. Yet he began his mission to spiritualize the West with courage and confidence. While living in a small room in the Boston YMCA, he told his first disciple, Dr. Lewis, "It's going to be big, Doctor. BIG, I tell you." And big it did become. Master saw the possibilities, and put out the energy to make it happen.

When Swami Kriyananda started Ananda Village in 1969, he had a handful of loyal students and only the little amount of money he earned from teaching hatha yoga and meditation classes. Yet nearly fifty years later, Ananda has reached millions of people with a model of a new way of life rooted in God. Swamiji saw the possibilities, and put out the energy to make it happen.

When we look at the challenges we face in our life or in the world at large, it's easy to feel discouraged, or perhaps even hopeless. The secret to navigating rough water, however, is to be aware of the rocks in your path, but to look for where the currents are flowing freely. Where others see only obstacles, train yourself to see opportunities.

Ask yourself: "What do I want to accomplish now? What positive difference can I make in the lives of others?" Look for the possibilities, no matter how small they may seem, and act on them.

Be conscious of what doors are opening for you, who is appearing to show you a new direction, and what effort it will take on your part to break through any obstacles. As our spiritual leaders have demonstrated for us, look for possibilities, and believe in the power of the divine to help you through.

Most important of all, meditate regularly to feel the flow of endless possibilities guiding you forward. In 1933 in the midst of the Great Depression in America, Paramhansa Yogananda gave his followers this daily meditation: "I am the mighty flood of peace which sweeps away all embankments of human worries."

So whatever tests come your way, ask God to show you how to use your own potential to overcome all obstacles. See the possibilities in every situation, until you know from your own experience that behind every cloud of gloom, God's light is always shining to show us new opportunities.

With blessings of light,
NAYASWAMI DEVI

12
March 23, 2017

FOUR KEYS *to* DEEPER MEDITATIONS

This morning as I sat in meditation, I ignored some of the advice I am sharing here. Instead of focusing entirely on my meditation, I spent some time thinking about this blog. (Ah, how often we ignore good advice, even when it comes from ourselves!) Yet I hope some benefit will come from my well-intentioned restlessness. Anyway, here is what came to me.

Keep your temple clean. You would be shocked if someone threw trash into your meditation room while you were sitting there. So, train yourself not to do this. Our true meditation room is our consciousness, so the trash I'm referring to is those negative, downward-pulling thoughts such as anger, greed, lust, or worry. Durga Mata, one of Master's closest disciples, said, "We are not responsible for the first thought that comes into our mind, but we are responsible for the train of thought that follows." When an undesirable thought arises while you are trying to meditate, don't invite him to stay as your guest, but immediately throw the rascal out. This is a habit that can be trained.

Sit still. Physical restlessness is easier to control than mental restlessness. Sitting still is not that hard to do: You just need to resolve not to move or fidget. Deeper meditations will follow.

Do only one thing at a time. Deep meditation requires one-pointed focus, so concentrate on only one thing at a time. For instance, if you are looking into the light in the forehead, do only that, just focus on the light. The monkey mind will resist this, so it needs to be tamed. The key is to bring it back under control quickly. Imagine an example of looking into the light for 1,000 seconds—a little over 16 minutes. You will focus on the light many more of those 1,000 seconds if you catch your wandering mind as soon as you realize that it has run off. Every meditator struggles with this common block to deeper meditation, so go easy on yourself, and don't feel guilty. Just catch your mind quickly, and then try to lengthen the periods of true focus.

"Eternity," by Nayaswami Jyotish.

Open your heart to the Guru. Never hide or shrink from your guru. He or she is an extension of Divine Mother's love and has only your best interest in mind. If you feel the Guru is judging you, it is a projection of your own mind. Of course, he will correct you, but that is different from judgment. If the Guru is no longer in the body, how will he correct you? Paramhansa Yogananda answered that question in his beautiful poem, "When I Am Only a Dream," one of his loveliest offerings. Here are a few lines:

> I will smile in your mind when you are right,
> And when you are wrong, I will weep through my
>   eyes,
> Dimly peering at you in the dark,
> And weep through your eyes, perchance;
> And I will whisper to you through your conscience,
> And I will reason with you through your reason,
> And I will love through your love.
> When you are able no longer to talk with me,
> Read my *Whispers from Eternity*.

Eternally through that I will talk to you.
Unknown, I will walk by your side
And guard you with invisible arms.

In joy,
NAYASWAMI JYOTISH

13
March 30, 2017

WHO ARE YOU?
TRUTH VS. FACTS

Have you ever been awestruck by a great work of art or a scene of natural beauty? The power of Michelangelo's "David"; the mystery of Leonardo's "Mona Lisa"; the perfection in architecture of the Taj Mahal; or the cosmic grandeur of the Aurora Borealis: I've looked at all of these, and felt deeply uplifted.

Yet when I try to understand them with my mind alone, when I search for facts to explain their impact, I fall far short. I can learn, for example, who made them, how they were created, or why they occur. But these facts have nothing to do with the power they have—this emanates from their essence, from the truth of what they are.

It's the same for each of us. We can define ourselves by the facts of our life—our physical appearance, our education, our religious background—but these have little to do with the truth of our being.

A friend of ours from Mumbai shared a beautiful story about his first meeting with Swami Kriyananda. When our friend (let's call him Ramdas) was introduced to him, Swamiji didn't know anything about him.

Yet, Ramdas told us with tears in his eyes, "He looked at me as though he had always known me. I've never felt so completely loved or accepted in my whole life." Swamiji was not responding to any facts about Ramdas, but to the truth of his being.

What is this "truth"? We *have* a body and personality, but we *are* the soul. Our souls are sparks of the divine and are inherently filled with God's joy and love. The truth of our being is this eternal, blissful Self.

Aurora Borealis. (Photo by U.S. Air Force Senior Airman Joshua Strang.)

In one of the most lyrical, inspiring passages of the Bhagavad Gita, Krishna says to Arjuna:

> He who is calm and even minded, never ruffled during pain and pleasure: he alone gains consciousness of his eternal existence. . . .
>
> This Self is not born, not does it perish. Self-existent, it continues its existence forever. It is birthless, eternal, changeless, and ever the same. . . .
>
> The soul cannot even be pondered by the reasoning mind. . . . Realize this truth, and rise above all sorrow.

Swami Kriyananda would often say in his lectures, "My goal is to show you who and what you really are."

So who are we? This truth is revealed through meditation and interiorizing the mind. When we move beyond facts and outer self-definitions to experience our own Self, then we know that we are all no more than reflections of God's unchanging joy, love, and peace.

Your friend in God,
NAYASWAMI DEVI

14
April 6, 2017

IS HAPPINESS
a CHOICE?

I would like to ask you to take a moment, close your eyes, and answer this question in your own words: What is happiness?

Now that you've formed your own idea, here is what Wikipedia says: "Happiness is a mental or emotional state of well-being defined by positive or pleasant emotions ranging from contentment to intense joy. Happy mental states may also reflect judgments by a person about their overall well-being."

Here is a second question: What would make you happy? Don't ponder this question, just get a clear picture of the first answer that pops into your mind. Most people will think of something outside of themselves; the largest group will probably think of money or something that money can buy. A smaller, but significant group will think of something concerning relationships. And a yet smaller group will think of something having to do with position, status, or how others view them. Any answer, however, that lies outside your own mental state is wrong. Things, people, position—none of these have the power to give happiness. But how we *react* to them will affect our state of well-being. So, if it is our reactions that make us happy or unhappy, here is a final question:

Is happiness a choice? That is, can you learn to control your reactions? The tendency is glibly to say, of course I can. But if it were that easy, everyone would be happy all the time. You would be happy all the time. Are you?

Here is what yogic teachings have to say about it. Theoretically you *can* control your reactions, but habit patterns from this life or past lives might limit your ability to do so. In order to be happy all the time, we have to change these mental and emotional habits. Patanjali goes even further and says we need to learn to *neutralize* the chitta (primordial feelings of likes and dislikes that reside in the heart area). When we can do this, we will achieve a state of union and a state of bliss.

So, what prevents us from neutralizing the whirlpools of chitta? Habit is one answer. Another is that we don't really want to; we still like the excitement of the emotional ups and downs of life's roller coaster. The first step is truly to want bliss rather than excitement or, stated another way, to want God more than the material world. Only once this desire is strong enough do we then come to the study of yoga, or scientific methods leading to union with the Infinite. And what are those methods?

What is happiness? Bliss.

Feelings, it turns out, are based upon the flow of prana (energy) in the astral and physical spine. An upward, expansive flow results in feelings of happiness and well-being, while downward, negative flows result in discontents and unhappiness. So Paramhansa Yogananda taught us methods that help us to control this prana, techniques of pranayama including Kriya Yoga. Day by day, meditation by meditation, we learn to bring this energy under our conscious control. When prana is in a still state, the waves of chitta subside, and we are finally able to see our true self, our blissful soul nature, which seeks nothing outside itself.

So, here are possible answers to all of those questions:

What is happiness?

Bliss.

Where can we find it?

In our soul nature.

What makes us happy?

To unite with our soul nature, which is already happy.

Is this a choice? Yes, but in order to make it, we have to overcome the restless resistance of the ego.

In the joy of the soul,
NAYASWAMI JYOTISH

15
April 13, 2017

LOOK *to the* MOUNTAINTOP

The faces of the young couple were radiant as we led them in their wedding ceremony in the chapel at Crystal Hermitage. The late-afternoon light illuminated the chapel's stained-glass windows, but the light shining from within the bride and groom was more luminous than the sunlight.

The chapel was filled with family and friends who had come to be with them as they took their wedding vows. Although the couple were relatively young, they were "old souls" who had dedicated their life to the spiritual path and to serving others.

As they repeated together the "Vows to God" from the wedding ceremony written by Swami Kriyananda, I saw that many of those watching were moved to tears. The vows begin with these words:

> Beloved Lord,
> We dedicate to Thee our lives, our service, and the
>   love we share.
> May the communion we find with one another lead us
>   to inner communion with Thee.
> May the service we render one another perfect in us
>   our service of Thee.
> May we behold Thee always enshrined in one
>   another's forms. . . .

The guests seated in the chapel had a variety of expressions as the ceremony drew to its conclusion. Two young girls, who probably had romantic fantasies about marriage, sat wide-eyed as they witnessed a different kind of love from what they had seen in the movies.

Young married couples looked at each other and smiled, as if to say, "Maybe we can take our love to a deeper level." Single people with sorrow on their faces, perhaps remembering disappointment in relationships, seemed to take hope and reach out for the courage to try again. An older couple took each other's hand and moved closer together, expressing their unspoken desire not to let their love fade over time. The beauty and inspiration found in the ideal of human love brought hope and encouragement to everyone present.

"We dedicate to Thee our lives, our service, and the love we share."

We need ideals to aspire towards in all aspects of our life — not just for our relationships, but also for our work, our mental attitudes, our physical health, our values, and our search for God. Without ideals showing the highest way forward, we can fall far short of our own potential.

As a boy, Paramhansa Yogananda had a vision of himself in a squalid marketplace in a town in the foothills of the Himalayas. Everyone there looked tired and dispirited. From time to time, someone would gaze high into the distance, then sigh deeply and mutter, "Oh, but it's much too high for me."

After this had happened several times, Yogananda turned to see what the others were looking at. There, towering above the town, he beheld a lofty mountain, serene and verdant. It was inexpressibly beautiful, and he longed to go there. But as he reflected on the difficulty of the climb, he began to repeat those same words, "Oh, but it's much too high for me."

Then he scornfully rejected this thought, and declared, "It may be too high for me to reach the top in a single leap, but at least I can put one foot in front of the other!"

Never abandon your ideals, no matter how completely they seem to be wrested from you. Your ideals are your guides to true happiness and fulfillment in all aspects of life. Take the next step before you, and the next, until you reach the mountaintop of attainment.

In divine friendship,
NAYASWAMI DEVI

16
April 21, 2017

FIFTY YEARS

Today is the fourth anniversary of Swami Kriyananda's leaving his body. Ananda Worldwide celebrates this occasion with what we call "Moksha Day," a day dedicated to Self-realization, or spiritual freedom. We start the day with a six-hour meditation at the Moksha Mandir, where Swami Kriyananda's body is enshrined. This is an especially beautiful time of year at Ananda Village, with Swami's beloved gardens filled by more than fifteen thousand tulips and thousands of visitors. It's almost as if he thought, "If people are going to gather to honor this day, let them be surrounded by beauty."

This past Sunday, Easter, was also an important time for me personally. My first meeting with Swamiji, an event that set the course of my life, took place on Easter Sunday fifty years ago, March 26, 1967. I was 23 years old. I had read *Autobiography of a Yogi* a few months earlier, and a friend had recently learned Swami Kriyananda's address in San Francisco. We shyly knocked on his apartment door a little after noon. After he had greeted us, he said, "I am working on a project, would you like to help?" As I eagerly agreed, I had no idea that the project he was working on would be me and my salvation and that of countless others.

Later we went to Golden Gate Park for a picnic lunch. He sang a few songs and told stories about his time with Paramhansa Yogananda. He wove in a few simple teachings; I remember him telling us about the qualities of the fruit we were eating—cherries were for joy, bananas for humility. I was utterly charmed.

I signed up for his next series of six classes on hatha yoga and meditation, and soon I was attending every event I could. Within a year I became his assistant, and we moved together to Ananda Community two years later. A year became a decade and then a lifetime, serving together.

Woven, like a golden thread, through the years was a precious friendship, love, and soul connection. We both knew that this was not the first life to find us together. I had been his son, physically or spiritually, in other lives, and our meeting on that long-ago Easter was not by chance, as it first seemed. Over the course of our time together, my life was shaped by him and by the incredible grace and blessing of Paramhansa Yogananda, whose light flowed through him so powerfully.

Here are a few of the ways our relationship has molded me:

I found out, once again, that the only true purpose of life is to find God.

The most important self-definition, the only one that counts, is to be a disciple.

I learned not only the techniques of meditation, but more importantly the attitudes that lead to success, among which are deep devotion, regularity, persistence, self-offering, and many others.

A life of service and caring about others leads to joyful freedom from petty concerns.

And finally, most importantly, I learned that gratitude opens the heart and soul so that God's light can enter and drive away the shadows that hide in the dark nooks and crannies of ego.

Words can never express the depth of my appreciation for a life with this great soul. Fifty years, even fifty lives, is too short of a time to share together.

In deep gratitude,
NAYASWAMI JYOTISH

THE NATURE of DIVINE LOVE

"I first met Swami Kriyananda when he began teaching classes in San Francisco in the late 1960s," David told me during one of the rare conversations we had together. An introverted, quiet man, David seldom spoke, but he needed no words to convey his deep, transparent devotion to God.

With childlike simplicity and joy, David went on to say, "Though Swamiji and I have only spoken a few times since I met him, he is my best friend."

What is the nature of divine love that can evoke such a lifelong silent relationship? I believe it's a beautiful blend of the personal and impersonal: touching the innermost part of our being, but at the same time dissolving our individuality.

In *Autobiography of a Yogi*, Paramhansa Yoganandaji describes his meeting with the great woman saint Anandamayi Ma in this way: "She seated herself with a childlike smile by my side. The closest of dear friends, she made one feel, yet an aura of remoteness was ever around her—the paradoxical isolation of Omnipresence."

On April 21, 2017, we honored the fourth anniversary of Swami Kriyananda's

Kriyananda with Jyotish and me in 1989.

passing by holding a six-hour meditation at Crystal Hermitage, his home at Ananda Village. Many devotees meditating felt his living presence very powerfully that day.

One friend told me afterwards, "There was a particular way that I always felt blessed whenever I was around Swamiji. During the meditation, I felt that very strongly."

As the hours passed during the meditation, I, too, felt the essence of how he related to me: It was mainly impersonal, but personal also in the sense that it touched my own soul nature. As I began to hold onto that feeling, I went deeper and deeper into stillness.

I began to understand that this is the gift of divine love: It is a love directed towards our soul, and by deepening our awareness of it we are guided towards the heart of God.

Yoganandaji ends his beautiful poem, "When I Am Only a Dream," with these lines:

> And yet when I am only a dream to you,
> I will come to remind you that you too are naught
> But a dream of my Heavenly Beloved;
> And when you know you are a dream, as I know now,
> We will be ever awake in Him.

In divine friendship,
NAYASWAMI DEVI

18
May 4, 2017

GLOBAL WARMING

We need more global warming. No, not the kind where the average temperature rises. I mean where the average consciousness rises. The only true cure for many of the world's problems—war, poverty, and even rising temperatures—is for mankind's consciousness to expand.

We are currently in the second of four ages or *yugas*, having entered the current age, Dwapara, a little more than three hundred years ago. As awareness, whether individual or global, rises, it also expands, and we become more altruistic, caring, and spiritual. As awareness decreases, it contracts, which finds expression in people's becoming increasingly selfish, greedy, and egocentric.

The problems trumpeted in today's headlines are all caused by contractive consciousness. The warring factions, politicians, and uncaring business practices are only expressions and tools of lower states of understanding.

Take water as an example. When its energetic state is low it freezes into ice. Ice can be cut into blocks that are kept separated. The human analogs of such blocks can clash with other "blocks," take over territory, and keep what is "theirs" for their own. But as ice begins to melt, it loses it separateness. Those who are committed to keeping things separate find this threatening, and try—more and more desperately—to "keep what is theirs for themselves." We are currently seeing this fear express itself all over the planet. We can't change the world awareness simply by voting for a different politician.

BE THE CHANGE
Sii tu il cambiamento - medita!

Take the pledge to meditate and be the change you want to see in the world.

Ultimately, the ice will melt, and there will be one undivided world. We are seeing this trend through technology and in the spread of increased opportunities throughout the world. As water heats up even more, it becomes steam. In this high-energy state, it can't be kept separate at all. Paramhansa Yogananda predicted that the model of the "United States of America" would spread and there would be a "United States of Europe," then a "United States of Asia," and, finally, a "United States of the World." We are already seeing some of these predictions come to pass.

How can we, as individuals, support this process? Our challenge, and responsibility, is, first and foremost, to undertake those practices that will raise our own consciousness. We must become the change we want to see in the world.* The most effective tool for this is meditation.

We need also to fight against contractive consciousness. We do this, not by meeting violence with violence, but by actively expressing the opposite, expansive attitudes. The beautiful prayer commonly attributed to Saint Francis† expresses this perfectly:

> Lord, make me an instrument of Thy peace;
> Where there is hatred, let me sow love;
> Where there is injury, pardon;

---

* See meditationpledge.com.

† The prayer was not in fact written by St. Francis. (See joyiswith.in/2.) An interesting tradition within the Roman Catholic Church states that it was written by William I ("the Conqueror") of England. (See joyiswith.in/2a.)

Where there is doubt, faith;
Where there is despair, hope;
Where there is darkness, light;
And where there is sadness, joy.

O Divine Master,
Grant that I may not so much
Seek to be consoled, as to console;
To be understood, as to understand;
To be loved, as to love.

For it is in giving that we receive;
In pardoning, that we are pardoned;
And in dying that we are born to eternal life.

The problems in the world are acute and now is not the time to be passive. We must all become warriors of light and instruments of peace. As each of us does so, we will become agents for global warming, not of temperature, but of hearts.

In peace and love,
NAYASWAMI JYOTISH

19
May 11, 2017

LIFE, LIBERTY, *and the* PURSUIT OF HAPPINESS

"We hold these truths to be self-evident, that all men are created equal, that they are endowed by their Creator with certain unalienable Rights, that among these are Life, Liberty and the pursuit of Happiness." This second sentence of the Declaration of Independence has been called "one of the best-known sentences in the English language."

Now, more than ever, it is important to remember the principles upon which America was founded, and to uphold the vision for a new kind of nation set forth by the enlightened men who created it. Never before in recorded history had a statement like this been made: that all people are equal; that they have a divine right to live in freedom from oppression, and to seek their own happiness. With exquisite simplicity the authors of the Declaration of Independence set into motion a wave of thought that changed the world.

For those of us seeking higher consciousness, we can take these words to an even higher octave. Life is more than just finishing out the days of our mortal existence, which inevitably must end. On a deeper level, it means to experience the divine spark of God within us, and to know that our soul is immortal.

True Liberty is not merely throwing off tyranny, but is a freedom of consciousness not bound by self-limiting thoughts. It means the freedom to follow the highest course of action in any situation; to choose to be happy in spite of adverse circumstances; to cast off

God's consciousness is reflected in all creation.

any limiting self-definitions; and to know your true self as a child of God.

The pursuit of Happiness doesn't mean only to seek fulfillment on a human level, but to seek the joy of God within us. Swami Kriyananda expressed this beautifully in The Vow of Complete Renunciation: "I am free in Thy joy, and will rejoice forever in Thy blissful presence."

And this leads us to the highest perspective from which to consider the words of the Declaration of Independence. In the teachings of India, God is described as *Satchidananda*, or "ever-existing, ever-conscious, ever-new bliss." God endowed each of us, His children, with His own divine qualities: eternal life, unlimited freedom of awareness, and inexhaustible joy.

God's consciousness is reflected in all creation: in the farthest galaxy, in nature, in nations, and in each one of us. We need but strive to see this, and to claim as our own the unalienable rights with which we are endowed.

Joined with you in God,
NAYASWAMI DEVI

20
May 19, 2017

GODLY QUALITIES – *a* CHECKLIST

Running through Ananda Village in Northern California are the rutted remains of an old road. A hundred and fifty years ago, during the time of the Gold Rush, when tons of ore were taken from the land around us, Wells Fargo stagecoach drivers urged their horses up and down these hills, and Pony Express riders rushed along carrying bags of mail. Interesting as history, but in current times this old road leads nowhere.

We all have the rutted remnants of old habits and attitudes that may once have served us well, but now no longer lead us toward our goal. Yet it is not always easy to know where we're headed or how to move forward from here. We need a roadmap. In a recently published article, Yogananda gave us one, suggesting that we develop twelve Godly qualities as a means of overcoming the ego:

1. Fearlessness and non-attachment

2. Absence of self-conceit

3. Purity of heart: no malice towards others

4. Perseverance (in the acquisition of wisdom and the practice of meditation)

5. Sattwic charity (including helping others materially)

6. Self-restraint (which leads to control of the senses)

7. Freedom from anger and faultfinding

8. Straightforwardness
9. Kindness
10. Forgiveness (giving a person a chance to reform)
11. Renunciation (primarily of the heart)
12. Tranquility in the Self

Take on only one of these qualities at a time so you can stay on task, delving deeper, becoming clearer.

It won't help much just to read over the list. That would be like looking at the menu of a great restaurant, but never eating the food. We need to chew, swallow, and assimilate these virtues if we want to grow strong and healthy. We need a plan of action.

First, we can read the original article* to more deeply grasp each of these qualities, and decide where we, personally, need to improve. This shouldn't be an exercise in guilt— we all have some areas that are more developed, and others less so. What is important is to be clear about our goals and aware of the hidden thoughts, emotions, attitudes, and habits that keep us from achieving them. Then, we need to get to work.

It is best to take on only one of these qualities at a time so we can stay on task, delving deeper, becoming clearer, until real progress has been made before moving on to the next. Each evening we can look back on the day, see how we did, and decide if more is needed. If so, we can develop a concrete plan of action for the coming day, perhaps even writing down our ideas and plans.

Fortunately, we have a model to follow. Today, as this blog comes out, is the 91st anniversary of Swami Kriyananda's birth.

---

* joyiswith.in/3

For me and many of us at Ananda, he was the living example, expressing each of these Godly qualities, often in the face of significant challenges.

These virtues are a part of God, and therefore reside within us already. We have only to bring them to the surface. If we develop these qualities gradually, day by day, then they will transform us into a beautiful reflection of God and bless the world we live in.

In joy,
NAYASWAMI JYOTISH

21
May 25, 2017

MEDITATION — IS IT HARD or EASY?

Our thoughts are much more powerful than we realize. In fact, they are often self-fulfilling prophecies: If we are preoccupied, for example, with thoughts of failure, we can draw to ourselves the very thing we fear. On the other hand, if we develop underlying thoughts of success, we can attract those things that will lead to further achievements.

The same is true for our thoughts about meditation—it can seem hard or easy depending on how we think about it. Let's look at some common problems people have that make meditation seem hard:

"When I try to meditate my mind is so restless." This is a shared experience for everyone who sits to meditate. As soon as we try to focus our mind, restless thoughts come rushing in to fling our efforts to the wind. In fact, in the Bhagavad Gita, Krishna says to Arjuna: "The mind is more difficult to tame than the wind."

But remember, restless thoughts are just part and parcel of the conscious mind: having randomly firing activity is what the mind does. The trick is to find that part of your consciousness that observes these thoughts, but is separate from them.

The more we can relax and observe, the more we can sit in a state of concentration, which is when meditation begins. Once when Swami Kriyananda was a new disciple living with Yoganandaji, he was struggling to focus his mind in meditation. Finally, in frustration, Swamiji asked his guru, "Am I not trying hard enough?" Master's answer was wonderful: "You are trying too hard. It's creating tension."

In his book *Secrets of Meditation*, Swami Kriyananda writes: "The secret of meditation is to send any vagrant thoughts in your mind soaring, like little balloons, upward through skies of Infinity until they disappear in the blue distance." Meditation begins to feel easy, once we can stop fighting the restless mind, and relax beyond it.

You already are those high truths towards which you aspire: inner peace, divine love, and perfect joy.

Another common problem that people share is: **"I don't have any time in my day to meditate, and if I do carve out a few minutes once in a while, I can't stick with it regularly."** There are some good solutions to these problems that can switch our thoughts about meditation from hard to easy.

First, analyze with honesty how you spend your time, particularly in the morning. Search for those extra five or ten minutes when you are lingering over your cup of coffee or browsing the Internet. Then make a commitment to yourself to USE THAT TIME EVERY DAY TO MEDITATE. Once you decide when and for how long you will meditate, stick to it. Meditation is a self-reinforcing behavior that will gain momentum as you commit to it. What at first seemed impossible for you will become not only possible, but eventually easily attainable.

Swami Kriyananda writes: "The secret of meditation is steadfastness: For the more you meditate, the more you will want to meditate, but the less you meditate, the less will you find meditation attractive."

Finally, why is meditation easy? Because the soul already loves to meditate. It's our natural state. Have you ever gone hiking with a heavy pack on your back? Remember the great feeling of relief when you finally took off that weight? That's what it feels like when we drop the heavy load of restless thoughts and body consciousness that we carry around all the time.

Meditation is our natural home to which we long to return from the foreign land of ego-consciousness. Swami Kriyananda writes: "The secret of meditation is affirming that you already *are* those high truths towards which you aspire: inner peace, divine love, and perfect joy."

Tomorrow when you sit to meditate, affirm that it's the easiest, most natural thing to do. Soon this will become your reality.

With joy,
NAYASWAMI DEVI

22
June 1, 2017

𝒜 VIRTUAL UNIVERSE?

Elon Musk is among a group of scientists and innovative thinkers who feel that it is likely that we live in a virtual-reality world. Their thinking goes something like this: The human race is very young in comparison to the life of the universe, and yet we have already advanced to the point where we are on the verge of creating virtual-reality worlds that can fool us into thinking and feeling that they are real. Therefore, the likelihood is that other, more advanced races, have already perfected this technology sufficiently to create a universe that seems completely real. And we are living in it. (Disclaimer: I am not endorsing this line of reasoning, only using it as a springboard for this blog.)

This approach answers a number of issues faced by science today, among which is a raging debate over whether the universe was created by intelligent design or whether it came into existence through natural processes alone. One great problem with

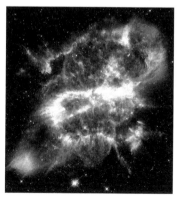

a materialistic, accidental universe is that there are a number of forces, such as gravity and subatomic attractions, that are so exacting that the universe would cease to exist if they were but 1/10,000 of a percent stronger or weaker. The explanation that some materialistic scientists give sounds more like science fiction than science: an infinite number of proto-universes all but one of which fail; our universe alone exists because, against vast odds, only we have won the cosmic lottery where all of these delicate forces are just right.

Interestingly, for those who accept a Vedantic view of reality the idea of a virtual universe seems quite natural. Simply substitute Brahma (or God) for advanced races, and maya or dream for virtual reality, and it seems quite familiar. In both views, creation is not what it seems to the mind and senses. We might think of reincarnation as the repeated playing of virtual-reality games, slowly progressing until we finally tire of it all. When our need to stimulate the senses has been sated, and we long to rest in truth, we begin to experience, as Paramhansa Yogananda described it, "an anguishing sense of monotony." That brings us, finally, to yoga and techniques designed to free us from the game of maya.

Similar though these two viewpoints might be, there are also vast differences. What is missing from the cold, alien virtual-reality picture is a loving and caring creator. Great saints of all religions, who have experienced unity with the infinite, tell us that God loves us more than we can imagine. Furthermore, that the devotee can escape delusion only by lovingly offering the separate self back into the father/mother who dreamt us into existence.

We, and the very fabric of the atoms, are made from love and joy, and our hearts will never rest until we are reunited with that reality. How fortunate we are to have found a path that leads us out of the virtual reality of separation and into the true, unifying light of God.

In love and joy,
NAYASWAMI JYOTISH

23
June 8, 2017

THE BEST WAY to DEAL WITH CHANGE

"All is flux."

"This world is in a state of constant change."

Down through the ages, enlightened souls have shared with us these truths drawn from their own realization. But we still expect, or at least hope, that the playful kitten will never grow into a lazy cat; that the vitality and dynamism of our youth will never fade; or that we'll never face debilitation or death brought on by the ravages of time.

Yet in some recess of our awareness, we know that life's changes are inevitable, and become distressed by the fact that things don't stay the way we want. A few days ago a friend of mine at Ananda Village shared an inspiring story about how she'd dealt with change in her life.

She and her husband are about to move on from what they've been doing for many years—the training and support of new community residents—and I was praising her for the wonderful job they'd done. Suddenly she looked at me intently and asked, "Do you remember how we started working with new people? You asked us if we'd be interested in doing this, and I replied that I'd think about it. But inwardly I was thinking, 'I'm dealing with some health challenges right now, and I really don't feel up to taking on a new job. Besides, I like what I'm doing, and I don't want to change. No, I'm not going to accept this position.'

"Change no circumstance of my life. Change me."
Painting, *"The One in All,"* by Nayaswami Jyotish.

"Later that day, as an afterthought, I added the prayer, 'God, I really don't want to do this, but if it's the right thing, then You'll just have to change *me*!' And I left it at that.

"A few days later as I was meditating, a wave of deep peace enveloped me, and I said aloud with complete conviction, 'I can do this job!' We accepted, and for the next eighteen years, I loved every minute of it—from taking out the garbage to cleaning rooms."

I thought about her story that day, and later realized how closely her words echoed the thoughts of Gyanamata, Paramhansa Yogananda's saintly woman disciple. Gyanamata wrote in a letter, "Late one afternoon, I was kneeling in prayer in the chapel—I was thinking of something that was coming into my life that filled me with apprehension. I knew that it was not the will of God that I should be saved from the experience. Even at that moment it was moving toward me. Suddenly God told me the prayer He would listen to, and I said quickly: 'Change no circumstance of my life. Change *me*.' My prayer was instantly answered. I was changed."

So what is the best way to deal with change? Follow the example of the wise: Give up fear of an unknown future. Don't resist or run away from change, or pray that circumstances be different. Instead try to embrace the only change that is lasting: personal transformation. Once this becomes our goal, we can stand with steadiness on the shifting sands of time, and find the purpose and joy behind God's will in our life.

Your friend in God,
NAYASWAMI DEVI

24
June 15, 2017

UNITY *in* DIVERSITY

I am laptopping this from the Seattle Airport, where we're waiting to fly back to California after a weekend of programs in Seattle. Airports are great levelers, as Devi and I know, queuing up for more than twenty-five flights each year. One sees people from all over the world: dark skin and light, baseball caps and turbans, families and friends chatting in English, Italian, Hindi, and languages we can't even recognize. All is marvelous diversity, but while at the airport we are all just fellow passengers. And so it is also on this little planet flying through space: we are all just fellow travelers. If we can but see the unity behind the diversity, we can all be friends. We can all be family. We can all speak the same language of the heart.

Good people everywhere yearn to see a world united.

One of our programs in Seattle included a Jewish rabbi, a Muslim imam, and a Christian minister, as well as Devi and me. At the end of our talks the rabbi led a prayer in Hebrew, the imam chanted verses from the Koran, and the Christian offered Biblical invocations—all for world peace. Many present had tears in their eyes, for good people everywhere yearn to see a world united in honoring everyone's common quest for life, liberty, and the pursuit of happiness.

At this transition point in history we are seeing a great battle of consciousness, between those who want to impose their small visions of an earth divided, and those who yearn for a world united. It's not a time to be passive. Those who want peace and harmony must radiate light: through prayer and meditation, by friendship to strangers, in a hand offered to those less fortunate.

Having lived so many years with Swami Kriyananda, I saw the power of friendship offered even when none was expected. Once we were in New York, where Swamiji was speaking at a large gathering of spiritually-minded people. The first Sony Walkman had just become available, and Swami visited a shop twice in order to buy a couple of these novel devices so people could listen to his music at the Ananda booth. He acted toward the owner as he always did, in a friendly and positive manner, and I didn't think much about it. But as we were leaving, we visited one last time to say goodbye to the shopkeeper who had helped us. To our amazement, the man began to weep and asked for a photo of Swami. He said that he felt he was losing his closest friend.

The world gives us back what we give out. Life becomes so much sweeter when we emanate friendship, peace, and harmony. If we want to see humanity truly reflecting the image of God, then let us act as divine representatives, becoming the hands, feet, heart, and mind of the Infinite Friend. Only when we see everyone as a brother or sister, a child of our same one Father/Mother, will we finally see true peace and harmony.

As Paramhansa Yogananda wrote in *Whispers From Eternity*, "Teach us, Father, to melt the fancy-frozen boundaries of family, society, and national identity with the warmth of our love and understanding."

In unity (from 30,000 feet),
NAYASWAMI JYOTISH

25
June 22, 2017

The SOLUTION LIES WITHIN *the* PROBLEM

There is a tradition among certain Native American tribes that where a poisonous plant is found, the antidote often grows nearby. It's as if the sickness and the cure are sister plants, expressing opposite sides of the same coin.

We can apply this principle in the search for truth, be it scientific or spiritual: the solution we are seeking is often inherent in the problem itself.

Our own immune system is a wonderful example of this, having the built-in power to combat untold numbers of diseases. The cure, however, doesn't become activated until the pathogen—the harmful bacterium or virus—is present in our body. Again, like two sides of a coin, the cure is linked with the disease.

In our practice of meditation we can draw from this same principle. Paramhansa Yogananda describes meditation as concentration on God, or on one of His eight aspects: peace, love, joy, calmness, light, sound, power, and wisdom. However, if we're in the grip of some negative emotion— anger, despair, or loneliness, for example—it seems nearly impossible even to begin to think about these divine qualities. But there is a solution.

Some years ago I had a very powerful experience along these lines. It was at a time when I was going through a period of feeling exhausted, discouraged, and, in general, overwhelmed by life. Finally reaching a low point, one evening I went out alone on a little porch, and began to weep, inwardly praying, "Divine Mother,

I am lonely no more.

this is all too much for me. I can't handle this."

Shortly afterwards I heard an inner voice saying, "Who do you think is doing all this? It isn't you, it's Me." The deeper understanding that God is the doer, behind my problems and within my solutions, banished my sense of facing this moment of despair alone. My discouragement and tears fled in that moment, and were replaced by a vibrant sense of well-being and command over all the tasks before me. I realized that when I had offered the problem up to God, the solution quickly presented itself.

In a beautiful poem, "I Am Lonely No More," Yoganandaji describes the divine presence awaiting within each of us:

> I am not lonesome in the chamber of loneliness,
> For Thou art always there.
> I am lonely amidst an uproarious crowd
> Where Thy silence slips away. . . .
> Away from Myself I was lonely—
> But since my little self met the big Self,
> I am lonely no more.

Many of the difficulties that beset us are simply what expresses in the absence of some corresponding divine quality. Here is a checklist to work with. If in meditation you activate these divine qualities by offering your problems up to God, you will find that . . .

1. Loneliness is replaced by **universal love**.

2. Darkness is replaced by **light and hope**.

3. Despair is replaced by **joy**.

4. Restlessness is replaced by a **sense of peace**.

5. The barrage of external noises is replaced by the one **sound of AUM**.

6. Mental confusion is replaced by **wisdom and understanding**.

7. Weakness and limitation are replaced by **power**.

8. Inner turmoil is replaced by **calmness**.

These are the antidotes—the eight aspects of God. Like a divine immune system, they are waiting for us to activate them by releasing the distress in our own heart. Only then will we find within the answers we have been seeking.

With joy and blessings,
NAYASWAMI DEVI

26
June 29, 2017

UNIFYING PRINCIPLES

John Ball was a highly regarded author and a friend of Swami Kriyananda and many of us at Ananda. His most famous book, *In the Heat of the Night*, garnered a number of literary awards, and later was made into a movie that won four Oscars, including Best Picture in 1967. He so enjoyed Ananda Village that the setting for one of his books, *Trouble for Tallon*, was an Ananda-like community.

Although primarily a mystery writer, on occasion he expressed his deeply spiritual side. One of his many books, *The Fourteenth Point*, departed from his usual crime genre to delve into a religious theme. It has a fascinating premise: A conference of leaders from the major religions is held, the purpose of which is to find a unifying statement that they can all agree upon and publish. After several days, they have to concede defeat because every statement of commonality seems to conflict with at least one religion's beliefs. Finally, shoulders slumped in defeat, they begin to exit the conference hall, when one of them collapses by the door. Immediately, everyone rushes to help and, a short time later, he recovers. They soon realize that they have stumbled upon a universally acceptable principle: the sanctity of life and the instinctive impulse to help someone in need.

As we drill down past those things which separate us, we find, waiting patiently, our innate spirituality. Past diversity, we begin to see unity. How could we not, if we are all created from the same one God? The other evening, during one of our monthly webinars,

a viewer asked a question that we often hear: "I like these teachings, but I just can't see how it is possible to love everyone."

If we are candid with ourselves, we will acknowledge that certain people or situations bother us. When someone does something hurtful, the typical reaction is to do something negative in return. But if we realize that disharmony is a kind of mental virus, we see that it is ourselves primarily—our own minds and hearts—that we infect whenever we are negative. And if kindness is a cure, then we heal our own consciousness when we give back love. When you are hurt by others, try to reverse the energy, for only light can dispel darkness; only love can heal hate.

If we search within for universal principles, especially when the mind and heart are calmed through meditation, we will soon find the right attitude. Plunge deeply into your inner self and you will find an ocean of universal love, deep peace, and unending joy. Swami Kriyananda said, "It is the nature of joy to want to share itself." After you connect to your own innate divinity then radiate it out: first to friends and loved ones, then in expanding circles to those who are in need, and finally, to everyone on earth.

When you have expanded your aura in this way, you will find it easy to send love even to those who have hurt you. As you do this, you can begin to shed the burdens of anger, hurt, and resentment that you may have been carrying for many years. Loving others, even though they are imperfect, will also help you to feel Divine Mother's ever-present love for all, regardless of whether they have been naughty or good.

Finally, when you are centered in your expanded Self, you will realize that someone who is acting badly is merely ill and has collapsed by the door, and you will instinctively rush over to help.

In freedom,
NAYASWAMI JYOTISH

The STRENGTH REMAINS

Some thirty years ago, my good friend Nayaswami Roma and I decided to run a twenty-six-mile marathon. Neither of us was a particularly great athlete, but we wanted to raise money for the Ananda School, so we took on the challenge and began training for it.

For several months before the event, we ran two miles three times a week, and then early every Saturday morning we'd go for a long run of increasing distance: three miles, then five, seven, ten, twelve, up to twenty miles two weeks before the scheduled run. The following Sundays were often spent dealing with blisters, sore muscles, and exhaustion, but we kept at it.

Finally the day of the "Joyathon" event came. Would we be able to go the distance? To our amazement, we completed the twenty-six miles (don't ask how many hours it took us), and were able to raise several thousand dollars for the school.

Recently Roma was visiting Ananda Village from Bangalore, India, where she and her husband Nayaswami Haridas lead the Ananda center. Reminiscing about our marathon, we marveled at the determination and will power it took.

We both realized that the physical and mental

Photo by Swami Kriyananda.

strength we developed through that effort still remains with us on some level, and can be tapped into whenever we need it. Once you cross a mental barrier of your own untapped potential, you always have access to that portal you opened, giving you strength and confidence in everything you do.

The same is true of our spiritual efforts. Every attempt we make to go deep in meditation when we're not feeling especially inspired, or to serve others when we're tired ourselves, or to summon up the right attitude when we're discouraged, builds a strength that stays with us and can be summoned at will.

Swami Kriyananda wrote a beautiful song called "The Hill That Was Tara," in which he describes seeing the five-hundred-foot hill where once lived the high kings of Ireland. The concluding verse is:

> And I knew in that moment, the deeds that men do
> Never die: Each vict'ry is true!
> Ev'ry effort we spend
> Gives more strength in the end,
> Till our gladness in life's ever new!

Dear friend, remember that every step forward you take on the spiritual path lays a permanent steppingstone to soul freedom. Strength builds strength, will power builds will power, and every little victory leads to final victory.

With joy,
NAYASWAMI DEVI

28
July 13, 2017

The CHANNEL IS BLESSED

Yesterday, after finishing some programs at the Ananda center in Sacramento, California, Devi and I had a few errands to run. Later, having finished our shopping, we were pulling onto the freeway entrance when we saw a family beside the road. The wife and child were sitting on a blanket, and the husband was holding a sign saying, "Our family is homeless. Can you help us?" Though we had but a moment to act, we lowered our window and gave them a small donation. But when we got home, Devi, remembering their eyes, remarked, "I wish we had given them much more," and I, too, had the same feeling. That evening we both prayed for them during our meditation.

In one of the more memorable chapters in *Autobiography of a Yogi*, Paramhansa Yogananda relates the story of a boyhood visit to the holy city of Brindaban. Yogananda's older brother, a disbeliever at the time, had challenged Yogananda and a friend to visit the holy city having no resources except an "unreliable" faith in God's benevolence. Soon, even after being miraculously and sumptuously fed lunch, the friend's faith began to falter.

Yogananda said, "'You forget God quickly, now that your stomach is filled.' My words, not bitter, were accusatory. How short is human memory for divine favors! No man lives who has not seen certain of his prayers granted."

Many people, perhaps most, never consciously pray to God but, nevertheless, He hears their every thought, every worry, every fear, and every need. That family, sitting beside the road, had been heard by God, and He inspired us to help them. If we had listened more carefully, He could have done more for them through us.

Worldly consciousness can find a thousand reasons to withhold aid. The devotee needs only one reason to give: because Divine Mother, in that form, is asking for help. Yogananda taught that the channel is blessed by what flows through it. Isn't it the better part of wisdom to be on the lookout for opportunities to serve as God's channel?

If we study the lives of the saints, we see that they hold nothing back. St. Francis gave away everything he owned; the Indian sadhu, Ramdas, gave a beggar the very clothing off his back; and Yogananda's "bank" consisted of a small box with a few dollars in it so he would have a little money to buy things for others.

In a parable by the great poet, Rabindranath Tagore, a beggar is sitting beside a road when the king of the land approaches. Expecting a generous gift, the mendicant holds out his hand. He is shocked when the king asks, "What have you to give me?" The beggar grudgingly gives him the tiniest grain of rice. When he returns home that night and empties his purse, he finds there a single grain of golden rice, and wishes he had given his all.

Subtle threads of divinity connect everyone and everything on the planet. If you see someone in need—not only of money, but of a smile, or a kind word, or a helping hand—realize that, behind the form, Divine Mother is offering you a chance to serve as a channel for Her divine favors. When we give to others we find inner freedom.

Give God your all, no matter whether He comes disguised as a king or a beggar, and you will instantly feel His blessings in your heart.

Widows of Brindaban who are served by the Paramhansa Yogananda Charitable Trust.

In joy,
NAYASWAMI JYOTISH

29
July 20, 2017

The ART of BECOMING

It was an Open House at a Unitarian Church in San Francisco where people could sign up for a variety of new classes. That evening I was sitting at a small table ready to register people for a four-week "How to Meditate" course that Jyotish and I would be teaching.

Two well-dressed middle-aged women approached my table and enthusiastically asked, "What are *you* teaching?"

"We'll be offering a course in the basic practices of meditation. Would you like to sign up?"

A little disappointed, one replied, "Oh, *meditation*. We already *did* that." They flitted away to the next table to see what new fare they could find.

We live in an age of extreme restlessness, where the possibilities for new activities and experiences are never-ending, but the ability to go deep in any one of them is largely ignored. People move from job to job, city to city, relationship to relationship hoping to find happiness in the "new."

Too late they realize that outward change does not bring what they seek, but merely repeats a variation of what they thought was left behind. The French have an apt proverb that describes this: "*Plus ça change, plus c'est la même chose,*" meaning "The more things change, the more they remain the same."

Without transformation of consciousness, external change alone won't make much difference in our life, nor bring us lasting happiness. "Change" may amount to no more than rearranging the pieces on the same old game board; "transformation" means changing how we perceive the game itself.

This process of transformation, however, requires inner discipline to focus the mind on whatever we're doing, and perseverance until we begin to change from the inside.

We might call this process the "Art of Becoming."

To practice it, we need to have commitment, patience, and steadfastness. As well, we need to view our life as a connected whole in which every step leads to the next, not as separate episodes with no underlying purpose or direction.

The world today is rife with restlessness. People are deceived if they think that a quick change in government will make a real difference. But there is hope, because world consciousness itself is in the process of transformation. It, too, is struggling to become more enlightened, and we can help in this process.

This year Ananda has started a campaign called, "Be The Change," paraphrasing a statement by Mahatma Gandhi: "If we could change ourselves, the tendencies in the world would also change." We're inviting people everywhere to join us in pledging a certain amount of time daily to meditating for world peace. You can find out more about it by going to meditationpledge.com.

Our potential to transform ourselves and positively to affect the world around us is much greater than we realize. When we abandon our fascination with constant outer change and focus instead on inner transformation, we begin to perceive our true Self.

This awareness of who we really are can't be found in time's fleeting moments, but rests always in the changeless, Eternal Now. In the heart of stillness lies the key to lasting meaning and joy.

Pledge your daily meditations for world peace at MeditationPledge.com.

Towards the one Self in all,
NAYASWAMI DEVI

30
July 27, 2017

FOCUS

In 2005 Devi and I arrived in India for a three-week visit with Swami Kriyananda, who had moved there in 2003. The day we landed, Swamiji had begun writing what was to be perhaps his greatest book: *The Essence of the Bhagavad Gita: Explained by Paramhansa Yogananda*. Though still playing the loving host to us and others, and despite the fact that he was in his eightieth year, Swamiji set himself the goal of writing ten pages a day for this book.

Swami Kriyananda at the completion of The Essence of the Bhagavad Gita.

To everyone's amazement, no matter what else was happening each day — and that included many hours a day spent with those he was hosting — Swamiji would bring his focus back to the book to reach, and often surpass, his self-created target. After less than two months he had finished the work: six hundred pages of fresh, inspiring insights based on Yoganandaji's Gita commentaries.

This accomplishment was the fruit of Swamiji's lifelong discipline of concentrating and focusing his mind. A friend recently sent us several statements by Paramhansa Yogananda on this subject, and I thought it would be very helpful to share some of them with you:

> "Concentration is the power by which you can free your attention from objects of distraction and place it upon one thing at a time. It is the gateway to power. The root cause of failure is lack of concentration."

> "Just as all human beings have eyes, so does everyone have a spiritual eye within the forehead. It awaits only your discovery by deep concentration within. If you can keep your mind focused deeply enough and long enough at the point between the eyebrows, you will get the right answer to any problem. The more deeply you concentrate your attention [there], the more you will find your ego dissolving into superconsciousness."

> "Habits can be changed in a day. They are nothing but concentration of the mind. Simply concentrate another way, and you'll completely overcome the habit. Concentration and meditation destroy mental diseases and corrosive bad habits that are lodged in the brain."

> "To acquire mental magnetism, you must do everything with deep concentration. People who have reached the top of their profession or business have great magnetic power."

Sometimes people wrongly think that spiritual teachings such as these are not very useful in the "practical," everyday world. But here is what two of the most successful men in the world, Warren Buffet and Bill Gates, have to say about focus. Shortly after they had become friends (each donates a vast percentage of his billions to charitable causes), Bill's dad asked them to write down on a piece of paper one word that best described what had helped them the most. Without collaborating, they each wrote the word, "focus."

Warren went on to say that he focuses his energy only on that which he is intensely interested in, calling it his area of competence. He suggested this exercise: Write a list of two dozen or so goals to be achieved within a set time period. Next, circle the five most important. Now you have two lists. The first, the longer one, is renamed: "Avoid At All Costs." "The difference between successful people and really successful people," he's said, "is that really successful people say no to almost everything."

We can best develop focus by, well, focusing. It starts with intention, is built by effort, gradually forms into a habit, and finally becomes a way of life. You'll be amazed at what you can accomplish by using the power of the focused mind.

In focus,
NAYASWAMI JYOTISH

31
Aug. 3, 2017

LESSONS FROM *a* DANCE CLASS

It was a sweltering summer's night, and the humidity in the air was so thick you could almost cut it with a knife. Young people in leotards and tights filled the second-floor dance studio, eager for the class to begin. Taking his position in front of the students, the teacher led us through warm-up exercises and movements. Soon everyone was feeling exhilarated, though dripping with perspiration.

True disciples always have Master in their hearts..

I had always loved studying dance and had been in classes since childhood. Two of my friends and I had signed up for an advanced dance class held in the evenings at a local university, and were enjoying the physical challenges and creativity that the gifted teacher brought.

"Watch the movements I do across the floor, then line up, and repeat the pattern individually," he instructed. This was always a challenging part of each class, because it required the ability to concentrate and inwardly tune in to different sequences that he demonstrated only once.

That evening after the teacher had moved across the floor in a particularly complicated pattern, I realized, as we lined up to repeat his steps, that I hadn't been paying close enough attention. I had no idea how to repeat the movements. Continually moving to the end of the line to avoid the embarrassing moment when I would freeze up in front of everyone, I finally was the last one left. All I could do was say helplessly, "I'm sorry, but I didn't get that pattern."

The teacher smiled, took my hand, and slowly led me through the steps, turns, and leaps. "Now," he said, "do it slowly on your own." I was able to do it, although haltingly. "Okay, now feel the movements within, and do it in a flow."

I could do it! What a joy it was to feel the freedom of moving in a pattern that had completely eluded me a short time before, and to make it my own.

Recently we were sharing with some friends about how a true guru demonstrates God-consciousness through his actions, and guides us inwardly to find that state ourselves. The experience in that long-ago dance class came to mind, with these take-away points:

1. **Be attentive** to the guru's guidance and teachings.
2. **Feel the flow** of his consciousness, not just his isolated words, to inform your actions and thoughts.
3. **The guru wants you to succeed.** If you come to a karmic block that you don't know how to get past, don't be embarrassed to **ask for help**.
4. **Follow his lead** and, more importantly, his inner guidance to move past the tests that come to you.
5. **Persevere** until you feel assured that you've tuned in to the guru's consciousness.
6. **Use this awareness** to build strength and confidence for the spiritual journey ahead.

Swami Kriyananda once said these words about attunement with the guru: "True disciples may leave outwardly for a time, but they are never really gone. They always have Master in their hearts, because this connection is put there by God. This loving soul-contact is the essence of what Master came to bring into our lives. You can get spiritual teachings from books, but what the great masters really bring is their consciousness and grace. What we must try to do as disciples is tune in with Master's consciousness, his loving presence and guidance, in every act of our lives."

With gratitude to the light that guides us all,
NAYASWAMI DEVI

32
Aug. 10, 2017

The CHALLENGES *of* LIFE

A friend wrote recently asking for advice about problems at work. His job is in a competitive environment where others disrupt the harmony, compete in unfair ways, and take credit for work they haven't done themselves. While this was expressed as a personal problem, it is in fact a nearly universal experience, to be found in families, governments, and, indeed, in groups everywhere. I tried to answer his question on two levels, first from the level of ego, and then from the spiritual, soul level.

Swami Kriyananda at the Kumbha Mela in India, 1960.

At the level of the ego, there will always be clashes of this sort. The less evolved people are spiritually — or, stated another way, the more attached they are to their egos — the more they will try to pump themselves up even at the expense of others. They are seeking to bolster their own worth, and will continue to do so as long as they feel the need to inflate their egos, which are inherently vulnerable.

Group dynamics get particularly tricky because, with people at different levels of maturity, the clashing of egos can get particularly turbulent. It is useless to expect others to be more mature than they are so that they fit better into the pattern of your own expectations. At the level of mass karma, such as nations have, generally the best we can do is to choose our battles and strictly monitor our own behavior to make sure it is righteous. Use common sense and do what seems appropriate, but don't become overly attached to the results. If you base your well-being on unrealistic hopes, you are destined to trod a long, muddy road of frustration and anger.

Now, from the level of the soul: Spiritual progress might be defined as the soul becoming detached from the delusion of separation from God. We should embrace whatever helps us accomplish that goal even though it may feel unpleasant. God creates an enormously entrancing drama, with grand scenes of good and bad, victories and losses. Our job is to take the road less traveled: to choose resolutely that pathway which leads away from ego and toward soul freedom. Here are some tools:

1. **Meditate:** Without meditation, the soul continues to be caught by the outward, downward-pulling magnetism of the world.

2. **Pray to God and Gurus** to guide your reason, will, and actions to the right path in everything.

3. In a calm state, try to **awaken your intuition**, your soul's intelligence. It is your surest guide. The longer and more deeply you can keep your focus at the spiritual eye, the more the right answers will come.

4. Always **act with complete sincerity and truthfulness**. This will enlist the laws of dharma to empower your actions. If you are selfish, unkind, or adharmic you will lose this power.

5. **Read Swami Kriyananda's short book, *Sadhu, Beware!*,** where he gives many helpful hints on overcoming the ego. You can find it at www.crystalclarity.com.

Finally, be content with your circumstances. Happiness or unhappiness is a series of choices that you make every day. If we understand, as Paramhansa Yogananda said, that "this world was made for our entertainment and education," then we can see that everything is, in one way or another, an expression of God's love.

In divine friendship,
NAYASWAMI JYOTISH

DOES SATAN EXIST?

Paramhansa Yogananda once said, "I used to think Satan was only a human invention, but now I know, and add my testimony to that of all those who have gone before me, that Satan is a reality. He is a universal, conscious force whose sole aim is to keep all beings bound to the wheel of delusion."

To understand his statement better, consider it in the light of another that he made: "All thoughts vibrate eternally in the cosmos.... Thoughts are universally and not individually rooted."

What Yoganandaji is saying is that there are universal thoughts, both positive and negative, that vibrate like radio waves throughout the universe. It's up to us to discriminate carefully and choose which of them we want to influence our lives.

Remember that both the positive and negative forces have their own magnetism that consciously draws us either upward toward divine freedom, or downward toward delusion and suffering. Satan has a bag of subtle tricks that can be all too effective in ensnaring us until we catch on to his game.

Here are some of his strategies, and counter-tactics that we can employ to be free of the power of negativity:

1. Satan convinces us that he doesn't exist. If we don't realize that there is a conscious force pulling us downward, we will wander unawares through dangerous minefields of "karmic bombs," negative habits from the past. We need to be vigilant and mindful of where we have gotten caught in the past, and exert will power to resist. People who have dealt with addiction of any kind

Every soul in creation must fight the inner battle.

know from experience that the thought "Just one little drink [or lie, or bit of gossip] won't hurt me" is the first step down the slippery slope to continued bondage. Recognize your enemy and fight back with will power and discrimination.

2. Satan makes us feel diminished about ourselves. Recently someone said to a friend of mine, "I'm a terrible meditator." Try not to hold any negative thought about yourself. This only weakens your will power and motivation to improve. Admittedly, we all have things that we need to change, but don't *identify* with your mistakes or flaws. See yourself as a child of God who is working towards soul-freedom. Remember always your true potential: a radiant being united with God.

3. Satan makes us think that we can hide our mistakes from God. But if we erect an internal wall to keep God's light from shining on our errors, we will only build a prison that traps us in a small, dark cell. Don't be afraid to give everything to God. Tear down those walls around your heart, and let God's forgiveness, compassion, and love shine into it. This is how healing on all levels begins.

Remember, finally, that God's goodness and unfailing protection, like radio signals, are always flowing through you. Every soul in creation must fight the inner battle to which it has been called, but the ultimate victory in this world of duality always belongs to God.

In divine friendship,
NAYASWAMI DEVI

34
Aug. 24, 2017

The ECLIPSE

Today, as I write this, there is a full eclipse of the sun. This rare event happens when the moon passes directly between the earth and the sun. Even though the moon is hundreds of times smaller than the sun, the apparent size of the two bodies seems the same because the moon is so much closer to the earth. During a full eclipse only the corona, the intensely hot outer rim of the sun is visible. Normally, this cannot be seen, but it is as if Divine Mother wants to give us an occasional demonstration of the precision of Her universe.

The solar eclipse of 2017.

Although this event is very interesting to scientists, astrologers, and viewers, I am more interested in its spiritual symbolism. The moon is often considered to represent our hidden, emotional nature, while the sun represents the outward-flowing life-force. Paramhansa Yogananda, in a fascinating statement, said that the physical sun is the *symbol* of our spiritual eye. The implications are vast, implying that the whole of the physical world is merely a symbolic representation of inner, spiritual realities.

When the moon eclipses the sun, the sky darkens, and when emotions obscure our higher nature, our minds grow gloomy. Emotions, especially when negative, have a unique ability to sap our spiritual strength. In Patanjali's *Yoga Sutras* it says, "*Yogas chitta vritti nirodh,*" meaning Self-realization occurs spontaneously when we are able to neutralize the whirlpools of likes and dislikes. So, how can we accomplish this?

It does no good to repress our emotions. That will lead to more problems than it solves. So, does that mean that we should freely express our emotions, no matter how hurtful? No, of course not. The secret is to transmute their downward-pulling energy into devotion or other practices that stimulate our spiritual zeal.

Yogic techniques, such as watching the breath or Kriya Yoga, help us gain control over the reactive process. Over time, meditators find profound changes in their ability to remain calm and centered no matter what life throws at them.

In daily life, you can neutralize a negative emotion by practicing its polar opposite. Love overcomes hatred, and joy drives out sorrow. Ultimately, the bliss of God neutralizes everything else. Life's lesser things fill our visual field only because, so long as we identify with our ego, they seem much closer to us. Once, Swami Kriyananda was lamenting his attachment to good food. Paramhansa Yogananda told him not to worry about it, saying, "Once ecstasy comes, all other attachments fall away."

Finally, realize that it is God's power that energizes everything. The moon generates no light of its own; it only reflects the light of the sun. Similarly, the ego is but a dim reflection of the soul, God's spark within each of us.

In the light of God,
NAYASWAMI JYOTISH

35
Aug. 31, 2017

HOW to CONTROL DESIRES

Recently a young man asked us, "Why do we do things that we know will make us unhappy, even when we don't really want to do them?" This is a universal dilemma, and one that brings so much suffering into life!

In the Bhagavad Gita, Arjuna asks this same question on behalf of all of us to his guru, Krishna: "What is it that draws me, even against my will, into delusion? What is that force?"

And Krishna replies, "It is the power of desire and anger, impelled by *rajo guna*."

According to the teachings of India, there are three *gunas*, or qualities, that permeate all creation. The first is *tamo guna*, the downward-pulling energy that darkens our consciousness and binds us to such states as violence, lust, and greed.

Next is *rajo guna*, which Krishna mentioned in his answer: It is the activating quality that keeps us forever restless and attached to finding happiness outwardly through the mind and senses.

Finally there is *sattwa guna*, the elevating energy that leads us towards the search for truth and lasting inner happiness.

Rajo guna keeps us in a state of perpetual discontent and awakens desires. When these are frustrated, as inevitably they often will be, we become angry. Thus rajo guna activates both desire and anger, the twin enemies of true peace and happiness.

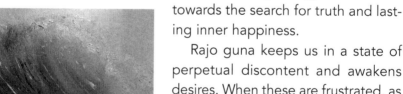
Rajo guna is the activating quality that keeps us forever restless and attached to finding happiness outwardly.

What can we do to overcome uninvited desires born of restlessness?

1. Be vigilant and watch the thoughts that drift through your mind before they build to become deep-seated desires. For example, you might think: "What a pretty car. I like that car. I Want that car. I NEED that car. But I CAN'T AFFORD THAT CAR. How frustrated I am!"

2. Counter little desires with will power and self-discipline: "That's a nice car, but the one I have is just fine, and it's all paid for. How happy I am!"

3. Simplify your life and get rid of "unnecessary necessities," as Master called them. When we can live our life in uncluttered contentment, we begin to tune in to sattwa guna and to enjoy inner peace.

4. Perform all your daily tasks with attention and concentration. Our duties can be the best opportunities to train our mind to become one-pointed. Studies of brain activity show that happiness and concentration are closely aligned.

5. Meditate and energetically oppose restless tendencies. Anyone who has tried to meditate knows that this is no easy task, but it is the key to success and happiness. By concentrating at the spiritual eye, we can burn up the seeds of desires before they begin to trouble us.

All of these are ways to take control of your life and overcome desires. As Sri Yukteswar, Yoganandaji's guru, said, "The forceful activating impulse of wrong desire is the greatest enemy to the happiness of man. Roam in the world as a lion of self-control; see that the frogs of weakness don't kick you around."

Towards victory in God,
NAYASWAMI DEVI

36
Sept. 7, 2017

BECOMING *a* GUARDIAN ANGEL

Swami Kriyananda was very drawn to places where Mary, the mother of Jesus, has appeared. One of these places, Medjugorje, is a pilgrimage spot for millions. When Swami visited there, he was elderly and unable to walk up the long, steep hill to get to the holy spot where Mary had appeared to the young children. In his chair, he was carried there joyfully by a group of six young men, whom he blessed in return. It was a deep and sacred moment in his life. This is a touching example of Divine Mother's love in action, but there is an even more beautiful back-story.

These young men, you see, were part of a group called Comunità Cenacolo (Community of the Last Supper), which has small groups around the world dedicated to helping young people with problems such as drug addiction or some minor scrape with the law. When a person enters one of the communities, he or she is paired up with a "Guardian Angel," a volunteer who commits to help that person for an entire year. If the young person is unable to do their cooking or cleaning chores, then the Guardian Angel does it for them, pulling double duty. If the person isn't able to sleep, the Angel stays up and talks with them, sometimes all night.

This living example of unconditional love begins to permeate and slowly change their hearts and lives. One key in the transformation is the commitment of the Guardian Angel for an entire year, which allows the time needed for growth and healing. As

their lives are reclaimed, and they grow stronger and clearer, many of these young people want to give back, and go on to become Guardian Angels themselves.

How often are *we* in a position where we could help someone in need? Perhaps someone reaches out to us asking for advice, or has an illness, or we know a co-worker who needs a friend. The next time someone reaches out to you, try to be aware that Divine Mother is giving *you* the opportunity to become a Guardian Angel. Open your heart to Her, and make a commitment to help that person in need for a year. But keep this a secret between you and Divine Mother so that your love and friendship remain pure.

People in need are often unable to articulate their needs or ask for help, so as a Guardian Angel you will need to be active. Reach out regularly with a phone call or a walk. Find ways to spend time together, helping with some little task. Better yet, ask them to help you, or find a way to do some selfless service together.

One of Swami Kriyananda's great secrets was that he made us think that we were helping him when, in reality, he was helping and blessing us. In fact, I wouldn't be surprised if those young men carrying his chair that day mistakenly thought that they were the ones helping him.

Angels work with love and joy, so let your time together be fun. When we connect heart to heart and soul to soul, we are both helped and healed. It is not surprising that, at the end of the year, most Guardian Angels report that they received much

more than they gave. That is why Jesus said, "It is more blessed to give than to receive."

Divine Mother will reach out to you sometime today or very soon. When She asks you to help someone in need, why not choose to become a Guardian Angel for a year?

With love,
NAYASWAMI JYOTISH

37
Sept. 12, 2017

The SECRET of a REMARKABLE LIFE

Today is September 12, 2017 — the sixty-ninth anniversary of the day a young man knelt alone at the feet of his guru, Paramhansa Yogananda. His heart aching with divine longing, the twenty-two-year-old James Donald Walters said beseechingly, "I want to be your disciple."

The Guru paused, then replied, "You have good karma. You may join us." Later at that first meeting, Yogananda said, "I give you my unconditional love." For the remainder of the man's life, he was shaped by that love, and by the consciousness of this great yogi. As a result of that meeting, many other lives throughout the world were destined also to be changed, as Yogananda began the transformation of his young disciple into the remarkable spiritual teacher, Swami Kriyananda.

Recently while at Ananda Assisi, we watched this touching first meeting as it was beautifully portrayed in the film *The Answer*. The movie, written by Swamiji, is a dramatic re-enactment of his boyhood search for truth, the predestined meeting in 1948 with his guru, and his years of training at Yoganandaji's feet until the Master's passing in 1952.

The Answer has already won nearly thirty awards at film festivals throughout the world, and will be released internationally in the spring. The movie's spiritual power lies in its depiction of the guru-disciple relationship, which opens viewers' eyes to the depth of care, wisdom, and love upon which this bond rests.

In bringing about Swami's inner transformation, Yogananda guided him in many ways over the years. Soon after Swamiji's arrival, for example, he told him, "You are too intellectual. You must get devotion." So Swami poured himself into chanting and devotional practices, until one day the Master said, "Look how I have changed Walter." (This was the name by which Yogananda always called him.)

Master placed him in charge of the monks, even though he was both young and new to the work. Under the Master's guidance, he organized the monks into a disciplined order.

Enthusiastically pouring his heart into everything that Yogananda asked of him, he more than fulfilled his guru's expectations. Swamiji gave of himself completely, holding nothing back—returning in full measure the unconditional love that he had received.

Towards the end of Yogananda's life, he made three significant statements to Kriyananda about what lay ahead. First, he said, by way of instruction, "Your work in this lifetime will be lecturing, editing, and writing." This Swamiji fulfilled, leaving a prodigious legacy of books, music, and recorded talks.

On another occasion he said prophetically, "You have a great work to do." What was this "great work"? The Master never told him; perhaps only with the passage of time will the full extent of it become clear. Surely it included in important part the creation of the ever-expanding Ananda Sangha and spiritual communities which share Yogananda's vibrations and teachings worldwide.

Finally, just days before his passing, Yogananda said to him lovingly, "You have pleased me very much. I want you to know that." These words gave Swamiji the reassurance and strength to fulfill everything his guru had asked of him, and became his guiding light through the many obstacles that lay ahead.

"We Are Thine," by Nayaswami Jyotish.

So what is the secret of Swamiji's life? It is the constant flow of grace born of total self-offering and unconditional love.

And what can we learn from his example? Few of us will leave so rich a legacy in service to our guru, but we, too, can offer every ounce of what we have to give. In the Bhagavad Gita Krishna says, "I accept even a leaf, if offered with devotion." No gift offered lovingly is too small or insignificant for God to accept.

Swami Kriyananda once said these words about Ananda's work—words that apply equally as well to him: "We are part of a great tide of loving, joyful energy that wants to give and give as long as people are happy to receive it."

Thank you, Swamiji, for your remarkable life, and Happy Spiritual Anniversary!

NAYASWAMI DEVI

The CRUCIBLE

I n medieval times, Damascus steel was famous throughout Europe and the Middle East because it surpassed all other types of steel with its strength and flexibility. Damascus, in southwestern Syria, became a center for the production of highly prized swords and armor. Their specialized steel-making process was one of the great industrial secrets of the times. It turns out, interestingly, that the ability to make this kind of steel probably originated in India, where it is known to have existed as early as 300 BC, and may even go back to the time of the Bhagavad Gita.

The method for making this special steel was to place iron and carbon together in a crucible, which is a type of ceramic clay pot that can be heated to a very high temperature. The components must be held at high heat long enough to allow the metal to melt and fuse and the impurities, or slag, to be removed.

The more sensitive readers are probably now scratching their heads and asking themselves, "Why in the world, in what is supposed to be a spiritual blog, is he prattling on about steel and swords?" So, for you poets and bhaktis, I am now done with armor and weapons. But before you get too relaxed, I have more to say about crucibles.

In life, some people make progress faster than others. This is true in school, business, athletics, and virtually any field of activity.

While some people seem to be born with more ability or in better circumstances, true greatness is made, not born. In fact, it takes many lifetimes for a soul to be forged into the human equivalent of Damascus steel.

Over the years of dealing with thousands of spiritual seekers, I've seen a pattern emerge. Those who allow themselves to be placed in crucibles—situations requiring the long application of fortitude and will—make faster progress than those who avoid challenges. Long periods of high intensity make these devotees strong and flexible. Eventually they are able to cut through any challenge life can throw at them. Heated to high temperatures, they become sources of light, giving love and support to countless others.

In contrast, those who avoid their tests gradually become weak and brittle. Not many of these can withstand the daily discipline required of a Kriya Yogi, nor can they last long in the crucible of a life given to God.

Given time, however, a more important quality emerges than merely the strength to withstand life's pressures. The impurities of consciousness, the slag of delusion, begins to be burnt away.

We would do well willingly to place ourselves into a spiritual crucible from time to time. Once in a while it is good to serve above and beyond what you think are your limits. Once a week it is beneficial to meditate for several hours. Paramhansa Yogananda said that the mind must become accustomed to the demands of longer, deeper concentration before it is ready for higher states of awareness and the tremendous flow of energy that comes in samadhi. And the heart must be made ready for the blazing light of Divine Mother's love that burns away all of our impurities.

In Joy,
NAYASWAMI JYOTISH

39
Sept. 28, 2017

The SPARROW, EACH GRAIN of SAND

She lay in the dust by the side of the road, alone and abandoned in her suffering. Her family had rejected her, and this poor widow had made her way to Brindaban, where an estimated ten thousand elderly, homeless women reside, hoping to find solace in the city blessed by the presence of Lord Krishna.

The large, malignant tumor on her back emitted such a noxious odor that no one came near her. Filled with pain, and having had no food or water for days, she prayed to God to allow her to die.

Then something unexpected happened. A man appeared before her and told her to go to one of the Paramhansa Yogananda Charitable Trust care homes. "They will help you," he said. "But," she replied, "I don't know where this place is or how to get there."

He clapped his hands, and a three-wheeler (small motorcycle rickshaw) appeared and drove her to the care home, where the poor widow was bathed and fed by the staff. When they saw the cancerous tumor on her back, they took her to the nearby Ramakrishna Mission Hospital to receive surgery and treatment.

After a period of recovery, she returned to the care home, where she received the loving attention of the staff and regained her health. A few weeks later, she came up to the director of the home holding a copy of *Autobiography of a Yogi*. Pointing to Yoganandaji's picture on the cover, she said, "This is the man who found me by the side of the road and sent me here."

We heard this story last week when we visited Brindaban to see the work of the Paramhansa Yogananda Public Charitable Trust, a part of Ananda Sangha's service in India. Started in 2014, and led by Ananda member Manjunath Kini, the Trust is quickly becoming a model for charitable works in this sacred city.

In 2014, Manjunath began with six dedicated people from the Brindaban area who were unfamiliar with Ananda, but felt a calling to serve the homeless widows. The small staff began by going door to door to see what help they could offer.

Now in 2017 the Charitable Trust has:

- eight residential care homes where food, lodging, and loving care are provided free-of-charge to 220 widows.

- distribution centers to provide milk and vegetables to 1250 widows on a daily basis, and monthly food staples to an additional 4000.

- a staff of ninety workers who operate the care homes and several small clinics, distribute food, bring the sick to the local hospital, and make about 2400 home visits each month.

These are all wonderful accomplishments, but what inspired us the most was Yoganandaji's growing presence in those involved with the Trust. Most of the staff practice the Energization Exercises and meditation daily now, and have taught these techniques to the widows, who practice them also. One third of the staff have taken discipleship vows.

Photos of our line of masters and of Swami Kriyananda are present everywhere, and the work is now becoming a "Paramhansa Yogananda" Charitable Trust in spirit as well as in name.

While we were visiting one of the care homes, an elderly widow came up to us with a question. She was reading Swamiji's *Es-

Staff of Paramhansa Yogananda Charitable Trust.

sence of the *Bhagavad Gita* in Hindi, and wanted to know why Krishna urged Arjuna to fight. How wonderful it was to share with her (through a translator) the symbolism of this great scripture as Master explained it.

In Yoganandaji's poem "Samadhi," he writes: "The sparrow, each grain of sand, fall not without my sight." Though we are often unaware of God's loving presence in this world, His eye is ever watchful, seeking to help those in need. Blessed are they who become channels for His love and compassion to the least of His little sparrows.

In God and Guru,
NAYASWAMI DEVI

P.S. To find out more, go to yoganandatrust.org.

40
Oct. 5, 2017

FEEDING *the* ANTS

We were staying at a little hotel near Rome. It fronted on a popular beach where hundreds of Italians came with their families: some swam or lounged on the warm sand, others jogged or walked along the promenade, and still others were there to see and be seen. It was a charming little slice of life. But early each morning when the beach was abandoned, a different scene caught my eye. Around 7:00 a.m. a car would pull into one of the parking slots, and an old woman would get out. Then she would reach into the back for a bag and trudge slowly toward the sand.

It was feeding time, and her bag was full of table scraps. From our balcony spot, I could see many cats start to wind their way toward her, some from a long distance away. How they knew she had arrived was a mystery. There was no obvious signal, so maybe it was the magnetism of her love. And this scene is repeated each day the world over. During a walk one time in a park near our ashram in New Delhi, we saw many people bringing food not only for the birds, but—to our amazement—also for the ants.

The human heart has an infinite capacity for love, and when kindness flows, we are not only uplifted, but often healed of some old karma. In the early years of Ananda there was a lovely young woman whose hands mysteriously became covered with warts. An astrologer told her to avoid any combination of garlic and milk and to feed the birds every day. Within two weeks, all the warts had fallen off her hands. When one's life is filled with little acts of kindness, it begins to heal not only them, but everyone they touch.

When asked, "What is your religion?" the Dali Lama simply replied, "Kindness."

Here in India and around the world, Devi and I are often told stories of how a kind word, or a mere glance, from Swami Kriyananda changed a person's life. We heard a story only last week from someone who had been suffering deeply from the loss of a loved one. She had tried everything to move on in her life, but was  unable to do so. At a satsang with Swami Kriyananda, he caught and held her eye from a distance. She said she felt a wave of love and blessing in his glance, and her heart was instantly and permanently healed.

There was a popular saying a few years ago that achieved a kind of immortality through bumper stickers: "Do random acts of kindness." In a world divided against itself in so many ways, the only cure is love. Love, being an eternal, divine quality, is stronger than all the bombs and hatred, which ultimately will pass away. Little acts of kindness, especially to strangers and the helpless, are the cure for today's divisions. Find a way to be a channel of Divine Mother's love, and your "karmic warts" will begin to fall away.

With kindness,
NAYASWAMI JYOTISH

WHO'S IN CHARGE HERE?

Two distraught devotees knelt before the Indian saint, Anandamayi Ma, pleading for her divine intervention. "Ma," they begged, "can't you stop this? It will produce so much suffering."

It was 1947—the beginning of the partition of India and Pakistan into two separate countries. The two disciples kneeling before Ma were government officials, who foresaw the disruption and pain that would attend the separation.

Source: www.anandamayima.org.

Anandamayi Ma listened to them thoughtfully, then withdrew into herself for several hours. When she returned to outer awareness, Ma lovingly replied, "Don't you think that He who created this world knows how to run it?"

World conditions today seem like a continuous stream of disasters, natural and man-made, causing much human suffering. From devastating fires, earthquakes, and hurricanes to mounting racial, religious, and political tensions—it's easy to feel that God is indifferent to our pain, occupied elsewhere, or even punishing us.

Yet in *Autobiography of a Yogi*, Paramhansa Yogananda writes that the great master Babaji and Jesus Christ are in constant communion with each other, sending out redemptive vibrations to uplift the world. Together they have planned the means of spiritual salvation for this age.

"The work of these two fully-illumined masters—one with the body and one without it—is to inspire the nations to forsake suicidal wars, race hatreds, religious sectarianism, and the boomerang evils of materialism," Yoganandaji writes. It's comforting to know that higher powers are at work and are focusing directly on the problems that confront us.

In a smaller way, in our own lives we are often faced with problems that lead us to think we must take matters into our own hands. Recently I learned about a situation in which the actions of a friend of mine were upsetting others.

This troubled me, and I asked God for guidance to see if there wasn't something I ought to do. Should I write a letter? make a phone call? I prayed: "Is there an action item here for me?"

The reply I received surprised me: "There is no action item for you, only a *reaction* item."

This answer made me laugh—for I knew it was true. I would only be reacting to what I perceived was my friend's wrong behavior: I wouldn't be improving anything. Telling someone else how *they* need to change is rarely a useful tactic. The action item was God's, and I needed to trust Him to handle it.

Watch this process in yourself. When we face a problem, sometimes there *is* an action item for us, and then we need to respond accordingly. But often we are only reacting, and not trusting that God is the one in charge.

When we watch disturbing news, for example, if there isn't an "action item" for us, then allowing our negative reactions to be aroused doesn't help the situation, or us. What does help is prayer and faith in God's supreme power in this world.

So, who's in charge here? The more we realize that it is God, the more we will find peace in our hearts, and be able to share that peace with all.

In loving surrender,
NAYASWAMI DEVI

42
Oct. 19, 2017

The DARKEST NIGHT *of the* YEAR

Right now in India people everywhere are beginning the festivities for Diwali—a holiday celebrating the reappearance of light in the world. Diwali commemorates the return of the avatar, Rama, and his wife, Sita, to their kingdom of Ayodhya after winning the war against the evil king, Ravana, and his forces of darkness.

Beautiful, elaborate displays of lights are seen everywhere during this holiday—on houses, shops, and along the streets. People visit family and friends, exchange gifts, and paint and clean their homes. Despite the great diversity of religions here, this joyous holiday belongs to all of India.

Interestingly, however, the date for this celebration of light is chosen to fall on the darkest night of the year, according to the phases of the moon. As the night of Diwali begins to descend, homes are magically illumined with tiny earthen oil lamps placed in special locations. One lamp is always placed at the threshold of the house, representing the juncture of the outer and inner worlds, or more subtly where our outer and inner selves intersect.

The spiritual symbolism here is multileveled and beautiful. In our own lives, God's light can often be found especially during the dark times of tests and trials. At the threshold of giving up all hope, if we light an inner flame of devotion, then God's light enters our heart and dispels the darkness.

In our meditation practice, if we reside in peace amidst the seeming darkness of inner awareness, and remain attentive at the threshold of silence, then we enter the realm of divine light and joy. In Ananda's Festival of Light ceremony, we sing a song by Swami Kriyananda with the words:

> Out of the silence came the song of creation.
> Out of the darkness came the light.

Mukunda (Paramhansa Yogananda as a child) at age 6.

Paramhansa Yogananda had a profound experience as a child one day when he was meditating. "What is behind the darkness of closed eyes?" he asked inwardly. An immense flash of light appeared before his inner gaze, and took on the form of saints meditating in caves. The forms dissolved, but the silvery beams expanded outward to infinity.

"What is this wondrous glow?" he asked.

A voice answered, "I am Iswara. I am Light."

Yoganandaji goes on to write: "Out of the slow dwindling of my divine ecstasy, I salvaged a permanent legacy of inspiration to seek God."

Diwali is a celebration of the light that shines through the darkness, of the victory of virtue over evil, and of the inner transformation of all of our darkness into divine consciousness. May it also serve as a reminder to us to continue to seek God always.

We wish you all a very beautiful Diwali season—now and until you are filled with God's light.

With joy,
NAYASWAMI DEVI

YOUR BRAIN on MEDITATION

I sat in a lab at the University of California in the early 1970s, electrodes attached to my head and body. As an Ananda member I had been invited to participate in an early attempt to study what meditation does to the brain. Ever since then I've had an interest in these kinds of scientific studies.

Last week I read a fascinating report of a study done at the Max Planck Institute. Researchers looked at brain changes resulting from training in each of three different types of meditation, and found that the different types are linked to changes in different areas of the brain.

In the first type, "focused awareness," participants watch the breath and internal body sensations, focusing their attention and bringing it back when it wanders. The second type of meditation involves empathy, compassion, and "loving-kindness" for others. In the third type, often called "mindfulness," participants observe their thoughts nonjudgmentally.

Unfortunately, Kriya Yoga was not one of the methods studied, but the path given to us by Paramhansa Yogananda includes all three of these types of meditation. Focused awareness is central to techniques such as Hong-Sau and Kriya. The study found that this practice "is linked to enhanced thickness in the anterior prefrontal cortex (PFC) and the anterior cingulate cortex (ACC), which are known to be involved in attention." The ACC generates expectations; when those expectations aren't borne out, it reacts negatively and creates a revised anticipation. For instance, when we expect a door to open, but find it locked, there is a pulse in the ACC. This goes on constantly throughout the day in a myriad of situations, allowing us either calmly to adjust or to become upset each time the world fails to meet our expectations.

Compassionate meditation was linked to increased thickness in regions known to be involved in emotions like empathy. On our path, when we offer healing prayers, send love to others, or mentally repeat an affirmation for world peace, we are enhancing these regions.

Mindfulness changes the brain areas involved in understanding the mental states of others and ourselves. This, too, we do in meditation after our techniques, when we relax and look into the light, or feel God's love and joy spreading outward from our center in ever-expanding circles. There is no better way to understand another person than to see him or her as our spiritual brother or sister or, even better, as a part of our own Self.

The brain doesn't *create* consciousness but only expresses it—otherwise we might actually die when we "die." Nonetheless, living as we do in this dream world, I find it interesting to see how consciousness expresses itself through the brain.

A major benefit of these studies occurred to me. So many people, including myself, tend to criticize themselves if their concentration wanders. This study shows that there are beneficial results from many different aspects of meditation. We shouldn't lose heart: Concentration, while important, is but one aspect of this wonderful science. So also are compassion and self-acceptance.

The important thing is simply to meditate regularly. As Krishna says in the Gita, "Even a little practice of this inward religion will free you from dire fears and colossal sufferings."

In joy,
NAYASWAMI JYOTISH

SECLUSION

View of Himalayan range from Abbott Mount.

Devi and I just finished a week of seclusion at a private retreat house atop Abbott Mount, in the foothills of the Himalayas. Ever-present in the distance is Nanda Devi, a mountain that many in India believe to be a living goddess. In this rarefied air, one feels the blessing of God and the Masters to be palpable.

Seclusion is a very important part of the spiritual search. In his Praecepta lessons, Paramhansa Yogananda wrote:

> Always remember that seclusion is the price of greatness. In this tremendously busy life, unless you are by yourself, you can never succeed. Never, never, never. Walk in silence; go quietly; develop spiritually. We should not allow noise and sensory activities to ruin the ladder of our attention, because we are listening for the footsteps of God to come into our Temple.

Time alone, in quiet, allows the mind to disengage from the world of maya, which otherwise entangles and entrances our consciousness. More importantly, it helps you to feel the *reality* of the spiritual teachings. Too often, our efforts and our devotions are scattered, like sparkles of light on a breeze-ruffled pond.

There is a lovely chant whose words are:

> Thou art my life.
> Thou art my love.
> Thou are the sweetness which I do seek.
>
> In the thought by my love brought
> I taste Thy name, so sweet, so sweet.
>
> Devotee knows how sweet You are.
> He knows, whom You let know.

Most of the time, amidst our busy lives, words to a chant such as this are repeated halfheartedly or in a distracted state, and are little more than hopeful affirmations. During seclusion, when my life really was given wholly to God, if only for a week, it was as if these words became living, emerging from the printed page and throbbing in my heart, my mind, my very breath.

Here are a few of the benefits I felt during the seclusion:

- My mind disengaged from activity and became quiet.
- Meditation was much easier, deeper, and more attractive.
- My heart turned almost constantly toward devotion.
- The presence of the Gurus felt very real.
- After a couple of days, the duties and problems of daily life faded into a misty distance.
- New insights, often very subtle, came unbidden.
- I deeply felt the sweetness, love, and constant blessing of God and our Masters.

Can everyone take a week of seclusion in the Himalayas where Babaji lives? No, of course not. But everyone can find a way to get away from the turmoil of life, to be silent and alone for a few days, at least. The memory and benefits of even a little of this practice will sustain you for long months as you trod through the hills and valleys of daily life.

Try it. Please.

In the silence,
NAYASWAMI JYOTISH

45
Nov. 9, 2017

The BROKEN SHELL

The boy's father was a harsh man. Constantly criticizing and belittling others, he was feared by everyone who knew him—but not by his son, who had a wisdom beyond his years.

One day when the boy was twelve years old, he came into the room where his father was sitting and picked up a beautiful shell bowl from a table. Lifting the shell over his head, he threw it to the ground and shattered it into pieces.

"What have you done?" his father screamed. Calmly the boy looked at him, and replied, "Can you put it back together and make it whole again?"

"Of course not," said the man as he approached the boy angrily, about to mete out punishment.

Swami Satchidananda at Ananda Village's Meditation Retreat, during a visit in 1973.

"Then why do you do this to other people's minds?" the son asked. The father's rage changed to stunned silence, as he realized, perhaps for the first time, the impact of his actions on others.

This boy grew up to become Swami Satchidananda, a disciple of the great Swami Sivananda of Rishikesh, and a beloved guru to many thousands of people around the world. He founded the worldwide Integral

Jyotish with Mr. Ramasamy (top). LOTUS near Coimbatore (bottom).

Yoga Institutes, and in 1979 established Yogaville in Buckingham, Virginia, where he built the first LOTUS (**L**ight **O**f **T**ruth **U**niversal **S**hrine).

Recently Jyotish and I took part in a well-received Ananda program in the south Indian city of Coimbatore. The following day Satchidananda's cousin and disciple, K. Ramasamy, drove us to a nearby town where he has established a second LOTUS. This beautiful temple is "dedicated to the Light of all faiths and to world peace," and is exactly two-thirds the size of the original LOTUS in Virginia.

As we toured the beautiful grounds and buildings with shrines dedicated to all religions, we were struck by the fact that the same consciousness is reflected in LOTUS and in the new temple being built at Ananda Village. People of universal sympathies are bringing the same awareness of global unity.

Mr. Ramasamy told us another story from the life of his guru-cousin. In the early years of Satchidananda's spiritual work in the West, many unkempt hippies began to follow him. Eventually he was able to uplift their consciousness, and many of them went on to make significant contributions in the arts and sciences, and in medicine.

At a certain point, a very wealthy woman began attending his satsangs. She told him, "I'd like to join your work and can donate a great deal of money, but [referring to the gaggle of hippies hanging around] I can't stand all these pigs."

Satchidananda smiled kindly and replied, "Perhaps this is not your place, because if they are pigs, then I am the mother pig caring for all of them." Unable to overcome her prejudices, the woman ended up leaving.

I'll close with a quote from this great teacher: "The real purpose of any religion is to educate us about our spiritual unity. It is time for us to recognize that there is one truth and many approaches. The need of the hour is to know, respect, love one another, and to live as one global family."

The broken shell could not be put back together, but the human soul needs but a touch of light, love, and understanding to, once again, be made whole in the realization of its oneness with God.

Towards world unity,
NAYASWAMI DEVI

46
Nov. 16, 2017

𝒯𝒽𝑒 MOUSE FAMILY

It happened again one evening a couple of weeks ago, while we were relaxing and chatting with some dear friends. My wife, Devi, who periodically over the years has asked, begged, or cajoled me to tell the story of the mouse family, prevailed successfully upon me once again. People always seem to enjoy this story, so I thought you might, too.

It took place around 1974, after I had built and moved into a geodesic dome. This was in the days before we were married, and I was able to be a little more casual with my interior-decorating motifs. The inside walls of a geodesic dome are made up of many triangular shapes, and it required both more skill than I possessed, and more effort than I felt inclined to expend, to cover them with wood, sheetrock, or some other type of fancy-shmancy interior. So I decided to go with the traditional, time-tested design theme of uncovered insulation. I freely admit that shiny tinfoil doesn't appeal to everyone, but in those days it worked for me.

One evening while I was meditating, I heard a squeaking sound coming from inside the insulation. It didn't take an advanced degree in investigatory science to realize that there was a mouse family living there. But this presented an immediate question: What to do about these unwanted visitors? Not wanting to kill or even hurt them, I decided to scare them in the hope that they would relocate to a different neighborhood. I stood close to the noise and loudly clapped my hands several times. Much to my amazement, the mother mouse ran out with a tiny baby in her mouth, about the

size and appearance of a pink bumblebee. I clapped again and she panicked, dropped the baby, and ran back to the nest. Carefully I took the baby and placed it in a wide-mouthed one-gallon glass jar.

The squeaking eventually resumed. Seeing how well I had done the first time, I clapped again and the same sequence of events repeated itself: clap; scare the mom while she is running with her baby; watch her drop it and run back to the nest; collect the baby and place it gently in the glass jar with its sibling. I was getting the drill down pretty well by now. Again I waited for the squeaks, and repeated the whole routine. After an hour or so, I had collected four babies, and there were no more sounds from the nest. I had corralled the kids, but how to nab the mom?

As I sat quietly, the desperate mother worked up the courage to try to rescue her family, and ran out toward the glass jar, which I had placed nearby. With a flash of inspiration, I carefully balanced a ruler on a strut of the dome and extended it over the mouth of the jar, forming a sort of bridge. The mother tentatively ran across it back and forth several times, retreating each time the precarious ruler started to tip. Finally she went too far, and her weight tipped the ruler, and her along with it, into the jar. I quickly put some grass in the jar, and gave them some much needed family time. In the morning I took them into the woods and set them free.

There are many spiritual lessons to be learned from this story, but I'll let you figure them out on your own.

In joy,
NAYASWAMI JYOTISH

WHAT WE SAW

There's a story about a young boy whose spirituality was so deep that he left his family to enter his guru's ashram at the age of seven. After some months had passed, his guru told him to go back to his village for a short visit to see his family and friends.

Global Ambassador Peace Award.

After the boy returned, his guru asked him about his stay: "Did you see your father and mother?"

"No, Baba, I saw only you."

Again the guru asked, "Well, did you see your brothers and sisters?"

"No, Baba, I saw only you."

Finally, with a gentle sweetness, the guru asked, "Didn't you see your playmates?"

"Don't tease me anymore, Baba, I saw only you."

Jyotish and I just returned from a three-month visit to Ananda communities and centers in Assisi, throughout India, and finally in New York City. It was an incredible experience, and here are some of the things we saw:

~

A true European Union of souls serving God together
and creating a spiritual community in Assisi.

~

A beautiful new "Temple of Joy" being built there
to serve the increasing number of devotees coming.
Hundreds of Kriyabans from all over the world
gathering together to deepen their Kriya practice.

∼

In India we saw shining faces of devotees sharing
Master's teachings and running centers.

∼

Deep gratitude and peace shining forth from
hundreds of formerly homeless widows in Brindaban
who are now being housed, fed, and loved by the
Paramhansa Yogananda Public Charitable Trust.

∼

Enthusiasm and joy in new devotees as they
begin to experience God's presence within.

∼

Increased inner strength and purpose in longer-term
devotees as they continue on the spiritual path.

∼

Beautiful, deep friends who helped us
in our travels along the way.

∼

Stillness and power in the Himalayas, and
especially in the serene beauty of Nandadevi.

∼

Glorious flowers everywhere—in garlands, bouquets,
hair adornments, floor decorations, and gardens.
Innate dignity and divinity in the people of India.

∼

Hope for world peace and harmony expressed
at the United Nations in New York City.

∼

And finally, the "Global Ambassador Peace Award" given to Ananda at the United Nations in recognition of being emissaries of Paramhansa Yogananda.

~

But what did we see behind it all? Just like the little boy in his guru's ashram, what we saw was the glorious, loving presence of God smiling through all of these experiences.

Now as we celebrate Thanksgiving here at Ananda Village, we are grateful beyond words for what we saw. We'll close with this gift to you: a note that Swami Kriyananda wrote during his last years while in India:

Dear Ones:

Happy Thanksgiving Day. Today is a big day in America, but what it stands for would be good for everyone on earth to celebrate: a day of thanks to God for His many gifts.

My undying love,

swami kriyananda

With gratitude,
NAYASWAMI DEVI

48
Nov. 30, 2017

BABAJI'S ADVICE

While we were in India, we enjoyed a wonderful conversation with Indu Bhan. Although elderly now, in his youth Indu was a key assistant and good friend to Swami Kriyananda. Indu's mother, Rani Bhan, was a remarkable person and a great help to Swamiji during that time. She was a powerful spiritual magnet, her house constantly visited by the great saints of that period. If you've heard the name of a saint from Northern India, such as Anandamayi Ma, Neem Karoli Baba, or Swami Narayan, they probably visited or stayed with Rani. She passed away in 2005, but Indu is still in touch with her through dreams and occasional visions.

Rani saw Babaji more than once during her lifetime, and Indu told us that she is still in regular contact with him on the astral plane. She asked Babaji a question that is in the minds of many of us: "Why don't you do something to stop all the darkness we see in the world today?"

Babaji's answer was fascinating and enlightening. "Darkness," he said, "has its necessary place, since creation depends upon the duality of both light and dark for its very existence. But although I cannot stop the darkness, it is my job to help increase the light." Good advice for all of us.

During our trip, we felt Babaji's grace more strongly than ever before, sometimes very palpably. We felt his blessings in Brindaban (Babaji/Krishna's city from ancient times), where every day Ananda devotees give material aid as well as love and dignity to many thousands of widows. We felt his hand behind the attendance of our talk in Chennai by Rajinikanth, the Indian superstar and Babaji devotee. He is so popular that sixteen regional newspapers printed the story that he had attended the event.

And we felt his blessings during the presentation of the "Global Ambassador Peace Award" at the United Nations. Shomik Chaudhuri, the man who presented the award, comes from a family of Babaji devotees. He himself received Kriya initiation at the age of twelve from a disciple of the deathless master.

Many other times also during this trip Babaji's blessings were present. And why not? After all, we have dedicated our entire lives to serving the work he started and still guides. He promised that anyone can receive his blessing just by reverently thinking of him.

But back to his advice about light and dark: It applies not only globally but also personally. You will progress much faster if you concentrate on increasing the light in your consciousness rather than focusing on dark areas that may remain lurking there. "The greatest 'sin,'" Paramhansa Yogananda often used to say, "is to call yourself a sinner."

One of the aspects of the yogic path that first attracted me was that it didn't make a big deal out of sin, seeing it as only a misdirection of energy, due to ignorance. If we but channel our energy in an upward and expansive direction, our darkness will instantly begin to wane. Master said that keeping your energy focused at

the point between the eyebrows, the center of light in the body, will fill you with God's presence, and is the fastest way to advance spiritually.

Forget the ignorant acts of the dark side and live in the light. Let's follow Babaji's advice and focus on increasing the light in ourselves, others, and the world. Happiness will follow.

In the light,
NAYASWAMI JYOTISH

49
Dec. 7, 2017

IS IT POSSIBLE to STOP WORRYING?

A few weeks ago we were having a heartwarming visit with our two younger grandchildren, whom we hadn't seen for many months due to our travel schedule. After enjoying their favorite pastime at Ananda Village — visiting the goat dairy — we were driving back through the peaceful, forested hills to our home.

From the backseat of the car, the little five-year-old said quietly, "I hope that they don't cut down all the trees."

"Oh, no," we replied reassuringly. "We only cut down the dead trees and the underbrush, to keep the forest healthy and prevent fires."

"I don't mean you," he expressed with a concern beyond his age, "but there are people who want to cut down all the trees."

I turned and caught the look of worry on his little face, and wondered what he had heard to elicit this response. The anxiousness I saw briefly in our grandson is widely reflected throughout our society today.

Whatever the cause, more Americans than ever before are suffering from stress, anxiety, and depression. A chiropractor we know said that in thirty years of practice, he has never seen so much physical tension and related illnesses in his patients.

What can we do about it? Is there something to break the toxic downward pull of mental anxiety and worry that is plaguing so many people?

Paramhansa Yogananda gave us some good, practical advice. First, he said: "Three times a day, shake off all worries. At seven o'clock in the morning, say to yourself, 'All my worries of the night are cast out, and from 7 to 8 a.m. I refuse to worry. I am on a worry fast.' From noon to 1 p.m., say, 'I am cheerful, I will not worry.' In the evening between six and nine o'clock mentally make a strong resolution: 'Within these three hours I will not worry. No matter how tempting it is to indulge in a worry feast, I will resist the temptation. I must not sabotage my peace-heart by shocks of worries. I am on a worry fast.'"

How to Have Courage, Calmness, and Confidence.

Yoganandaji concluded by saying that after you succeed in worry fasting for certain hours of the day, try to do it for one or two weeks at a time. He also encouraged us in these three other practices:

1. Feast regularly on the society of those with joyful minds until your mind is filled with sunshine.

2. Perform tirelessly right actions without concern for their results.

3. Drink copiously from the fresh waters of peace, vitalized by your determination to be cheerful under all circumstances.

As lighthearted as these suggestions may seem, are they easy to put into practice? Of course not: It takes all of our focus and will power to succeed in overcoming worries. But remember, we have a hidden ally in our Divine Friend. Yoganandaji wrote in his poem, "God! God! God!":

> When boisterous storms of trials shriek,
> And when worries howl at me,
> I will drown their noises, loudly chanting:
> God! God! God!

Following the teachings of the great spiritual teachers, there is so much we can do to transform our own consciousness and also to help others. Shall we begin together?

With joy,
NAYASWAMI DEVI

50
Dec. 14, 2017

GOD, GURUS, GURUBHAIS, *and* GRIT

Next week I will celebrate two important milestones. December 22 will be the fiftieth anniversary of my first Kriya Initiation. The next day will be another fiftieth anniversary: of my first eight-hour Christmas meditation. Both of these events took place in Swami Kriyananda's little apartment in San Francisco in 1967. I had been with him for about eight months when he told me, "I think you should take Kriya initiation."

"Do you think I'm ready?" I asked.

"Yes, I think it will be good for you. And also, you will be able to practice Kriya during the long meditation the next day."

So that evening fifty years ago, a newborn disciple took his first Kriya breath. I have been practicing it daily all these many years. I suppose that somewhere in the Akashic records there might be a counting of all the meditations and all the Kriya breaths that have transpired since that first evening. But numbers, either of years or of breaths offered, fade away in the remembrance of a lifetime of grace that has been showered upon this humble devotee.

Over time, Swamiji's little apartment in San Francisco has grown to hundreds of centers and communities around the world. And that handful of meditators has grown to hundreds of thousands who now draw inspiration from Ananda and our great gurus. Though there has been extraordinary growth, the enduring qualities that filled Swamiji's apartment are with us still: devotion, meditation, Kriya Yoga, satsang, and service.

As far as I know, out of those present at that first Kriya Initiation, only I remain a devotee. A few have been taken by the angel of death; others have been blown from the path by the storms of karma. So, what does it take to get to the fifty-year mark?

First, it takes the grace of God. Paramhansa Yogananda said that fifty percent of our progress is due to God's grace. This grace is eternally present and free for the taking; we must for our part simply be willing to let it fill our hearts and lives.

Secondly, Master said that the guru's blessings account for another twenty-five percent. Our great line of gurus have given us not only techniques and teachings but, more importantly, their love and magnetism. Again, it is given freely. You have but to hold out your hands to receive.

The last twenty-five percent is supplied by our own efforts: by our sadhana and our service. These efforts must be applied diligently and persistently. It takes a certain amount of grit, of stubborn determination, to stay faithful to our higher aspirations. There are good days and bad, times when meditation is easy and other times when the path seems as dry as desert sands. You must learn to brush aside outer conditions: to fly when you can, but, when your tests come, to plod along undeterred.

It is immensely helpful to have the support and magnetism of gurubhais. I remember a quote by Ratan Tata, the great Indian industrialist: "If you want to walk fast, walk alone. If you want to walk far, walk with others." The best trekking companions, those who will walk by your side to the very end, are God, Gurus, and your devotee friends.

This morning during meditation, as I remembered those long-ago events, my eyes filled with tears of gratitude. What a wonderful life we have been given.

In God's love,

NAYASWAMI JYOTISH

"Holy Night," by Nayaswami Jyotish.

The SHAWL of GOLD

The three kings from the East visit the Holy Family in Bethlehem. Stained glass in a Brussels cathedral.

Recently we attended a Christmas concert here at Ananda Village which was resplendent in its simplicity, with beautiful pieces by Swami Kriyananda as well as some traditional carols. I wasn't raised a Christian, but somehow love for Christ has always been a part of me. For as long as I can remember I've felt special blessings at Christmastime: a unique combination of humility and gentleness, as well as infinite kindness, compassion, and love.

During the concert last week, two of our gifted musicians performed Swamiji's song, "The Shawl of Gold."* It tells the story of a poor girl on a cold, wintry night who approaches a rich man about to enter a church, to ask him for help in finding work. He pompously sends this "impious girl" off into the frigid night.

As she wanders forlornly away, she spies a little boy even poorer than herself huddled against a doorway. Feeling deep compassion, she gives him the only thing she has to spare—her threadbare shawl. And then a miracle takes place.

---

* You can listen to (or download) the song at joyiswith.in/4. Swami Kriyananda was ever new, and just months before his passing he made a number of changes to his song lyrics. No time remained to him to record the new versions, however. Others have recorded those, but we thought you might enjoy hearing Swamiji himself sing the song.

She and the small boy are encircled by warmth, and she hears a tender voice comforting and reassuring her that all their needs will be met.

The voice then says:

> My child, all men's sorrows would turn to joy,
> If they knew that to share is no loss.
> For it's kindness broadens the human heart:
> I know, I who died on the cross!

I've heard this song many times over the years. Often it has brought tears to my eyes as I feel the simple yet infinite love that is Christ Consciousness.

In this holiday season, let's all remember the true meaning of Christmas as symbolized by this beautiful song. We are here on earth to learn how to love as the great masters love: with no thought of self; no concern for personal gain or loss; no barriers towards others, be they wise or foolish.

Swami Kriyananda sent a Christmas letter to Ananda in 1987, in which he shared this inspiration that had come to him during a just-completed period of seclusion:

> Love all mankind in God! Become transformed, not only *by* His love, but *into* His love! It is not enough to hold this divine inspiration of love as your own secret treasure. Let God, through you, reach out and touch the hearts of all!

Let us help bring the Christ Consciousness down to earth by giving whatever we can to others: a smile, perhaps; a comforting word; or a gift to someone alone and unremembered. Let's give our threadbare cloak of love to another in need, and, like the little girl in the song, see how God transforms it into a shawl of fine gold.

With joy in God, Christ, and Guru,
NAYASWAMI DEVI

RESOLUTIONS

The tide of the old year is ebbing, and the new one is rolling in. It is time, once again, for New Year's resolutions: the best opportunity to rid yourself of those habits you know to be self-destructive, and to develop those that you know will improve your life.

Paramhansa Yogananda regularly wrote his students at this time of year, encouraging, supporting, and strengthening them in their resolutions. Here is an excerpt from a 1937 letter:

> Take all the salvaged treasures of good experiences from the sea of past experience and use them to buy new accomplishments in the New Year. In the garden of the New Year culture the seeds of well-planned new activities until they grow into fragrant flowering plants of diverse successes. Let every day in the New Year become a step upward on the ladder of your Self-realization. Make every day of the New Year a better day than the previous one for greater effort to succeed in business, family happiness, and increasing the ever-new joy-contact of God in meditation. The old year has gone, but the New Year is full of treasures for you to use.

The real key is to nurture a new resolution long enough for it to grow into a "fragrant flowering plant." This is where most people fail, and why you find those springtime ads that read, "Treadmill, nearly new, used only twice. Half price."

Nurture a new resolution long enough for it to grow into a "fragrant flowering plant."

We were told a joke by a doctor friend: A man comes to a doctor complaining about pain in his body. "Doctor, it hurts when I touch my knee. It hurts when I touch my elbow, or my jaw, or my forehead." After an examination, the doctor says, "Your knee is fine, your elbow is fine, and so are your jaw and forehead. The problem is that you have a broken finger."

So often, we neglect the underlying cause. The difficulty doesn't lie with not exercising, or eating too much sugar, or not meditating enough. The problem lies with our will power: the creator and destroyer of habits. If it breaks easily, it is the finger that causes the pain in our life. When we strengthen it, we begin to fix all our other, more superficial problems. So, how do we bolster our will power? Here are five key ways:

1. Take on only one or two things at a time, those that you really want to accomplish. I would suggest that you choose one physical habit, let's say exercise, and one spiritual habit, such as meditation.

2. Translate a vague resolution into a very specific action item: "I will walk (or meditate) for 45 minutes every morning."

3. Most importantly, stay with it long enough for the old habit to fall away and a new habit to form. Don't allow yourself any "wiggle room" for at least one month.

4. Find a partner who is trying to accomplish the same thing. You will help each other through the inevitable low points.

5. Pray to God and Gurus to add their support to your good efforts.

Finally, remember to have fun with life. Will power doesn't need to be grim. Rather, let it be a joyful flow of energy helping to accomplish your chosen goals. As Swami Kriyananda says, "Joy is the solution, not the reward." This would be a good motto for the new year.

With joy,
NAYASWAMI JYOTISH

FINDING YOUR OWN SPIRITUAL POWER *in* 2018

Today, January 5, we celebrate the birthday of Paramhansa Yogananda, who brought to earth the spiritual power to uplift humanity. In one of the most amazing passages in *Autobiography of a Yogi*, he describes his experience of cosmic consciousness: "A swelling glory within me began to envelop towns, continents, the earth, solar and stellar systems, tenuous nebulae, and floating universes. . . . I cognized the center of the empyrean as a point of intuitive perception in my heart."

If the center of the universe lies within us, then there is a reservoir of strength we can draw on! We can access it by developing, through deep meditation, our inner connection with God — the source of all power. The stronger this connection grows, the more our fears and anxieties melt away.

Spiritual power is not ours to grasp or own, but will flow through us if we act in accordance with God's will. It isn't about controlling others, or defeating and destroying them — that is the realm of worldly power.

When Jesus Christ was taken by the Roman soldiers to be tried and crucified, his disciples drew their swords to defend him. He stayed their hands, saying, "Thinkest thou that I cannot now pray to my Father,

Photo by NASA.

and he shall presently give me more than twelve legions of angels? But how then shall the scriptures be fulfilled, that thus it must be?" Certainly he had the power to destroy his attackers, but he chose to use his strength to do the will of God.

Yoganandaji said that every test we face in life is a test of our will power, and that we are never given a test that we don't have the ability to overcome. Once we understand these two points, we are armed with powerful weapons to lead us to victory.

Spiritual power also enables us to become a source of strength and hope for others. In his life Swami Kriyananda was faced with test after test, but with a strength drawn from his faith in God and attunement with his guru, he was able to overcome every obstacle in his path. The creation of Ananda, and the hundreds of thousands brought to Yogananda's path through it, are ample testament to what spiritual power can accomplish.

Once, after Swamiji had gone through a particularly difficult period, I said to him, "I don't know if I have the strength to endure what you've had to go through in this lifetime."

"I didn't know that I had the strength," he replied, "but faith is my armor." So powerful was this statement that I used it as the title for a biography of his life—*Faith Is My Armor*—that he asked me several years later to write.

Recently I read an essay called, "We Were Made for These Times." It concluded with the words: "When a great ship is in harbor and moored, it is safe, there can be no doubt. But that is not what great ships are built for."

So as you embark on the voyage of 2018, whatever obstacles may lie before you, remember to draw on the examples of the great spiritual warriors. Like them, develop your own spiritual power so that you can sail safely through all of life's storms, and steer your soul ship to the shores of God-consciousness.

Wishing you a blessed New Year,
NAYASWAMI DEVI

TEAMWORK

Cooperation, being able to work as part of a team, is an essential skill in life. While this is true in business, sports, or any other undertaking, it is also important spiritually, where aligning our individual will with God's will is a vital step on the spiral stairway that leads to Self-realization.

In a practical sense, teamwork is needed if we want to accomplish tasks beyond the scope of a single individual. There are certain stages to forming a team. The first step is to have a very clear goal. Each sport, for instance, has rules and a purpose that are well defined. If the goal is clear and simple, sometimes a team can form more or less spontaneously. I remember how, when I was young, the boys in our neighborhood would come together and quickly sort out our roles in whatever game we were playing that day. But of course as the games we play become more serious and complex, we can't rely on simple spontaneity. We need a coach or manager.

A good manager needs to make sure that the goal or purpose is clear, be able to articulate it lucidly, and, most importantly, get everyone on the team to "buy in." A friend who spent a career managing teams for the internet company LinkedIn told us that they described the process of team formation with this phrase: "Forming, storming, norming, and performing."

"Forming" is when the team comes together. "Storming" is the next stage, when the various members are sorting out their roles and responsibilities. This can get particularly tricky when a new leader comes into an existing team, where people with old roles and loyalties might be reluctant to change. "Norming" is when everyone finally accepts and settles into their role and the team is at last ready to start. "Performing" is doing the job.

Cooperation to begin building a Temple of Joy in Assisi, Italy.

Once this last stage has been reached, the leader needs to keep everyone focused, coordinated, and inspired. In a spiritual organization such as Ananda, there is the added obligation of keeping the operation in tune with the true leader, God or Guru.

This whole topic may seem to have drifted a bit from a spiritual focus, but cooperation is essential also to our spiritual growth. Swami Kriyananda created a simple Discipleship Ceremony for those ready to become disciples of our line of gurus. It has a vow that includes these lines: "I will join my energies to those of my gurubhais, my spiritual family on earth. I will cooperate with them, and especially with the living representatives and guides of my divine line of gurus." Ultimately, being able to join your energies with others' is a steppingstone to being able to surrender your ego to God.

Yogananda compared our various thoughts to "mental citizens." When we sit to meditate we need our thought citizens to form a team committed to the goal of union with the Divine. Just this morning, as I sat to meditate, I became aware that there was a rowdy gang, probably cranky from having to get up early, which wanted no part of the discipline of watching the breath. With repeated effort, bringing my mind back when it wandered, I was able to get them to "join their energies to those of their gurubhais." As we all became more focused on the goal of stilling what Yogananda called "the twin tumults of breath and mind," I could feel my heart and soul expanding and getting more in tune with

God and my own divine nature. Only then could my innate love and joy begin to percolate to the surface of my consciousness.

Yes, teamwork is needed on all levels, and can accomplish miracles.

In joy,
NAYASWAMI JYOTISH

TOUCHING *the* SILENCE

> "My silence, like an expanding sphere, spreads everywhere. My silence spreads like a radio song, above, beneath, left and right, within and without."
>
> – *Paramhansa Yogananda*

Last Saturday was a beautiful, sunny day, and I was enjoying a walk alone through the quiet forest paths of Ananda Village. Suddenly, in a secluded area, I came upon one of our residents hard at work clearing underbrush — an essential job when you live in an area prone to forest fires. With his loppers (long-bladed hand shears), Ramdas was removing great quantities of Scotch broom, an invasive, highly flammable shrub.

"Thanks for doing this," I said in appreciation for his volunteer service.

Ramdas looked up at me and simply said, "It's so quiet and peaceful here."

Up to that point, I'd been walking along silently, but my mind had been busy with an active flow of thoughts. Hearing his words, I tuned in to the quiet and peace that he was experiencing. It was deep and refreshing, and had been there all along, but my internal conversation had blocked it out. The silence remained with me for the rest of the walk.

A friend of mine, Premi, who teaches second grade at an Ananda Living Wisdom School, told me about an experience that her class had had with practicing silence. Returning to school to begin their second term, she'd invited the children to write down goals for the class and stick them on a "Tower of Will Power" that she had created. One very active boy with a magnetic personality surprised her by saying, "Let's meditate for five minutes every day."

The class had never meditated together, but everyone agreed to try it. Premi told them that they were free to stop at any time, but should remain quiet out of respect for the others. Sitting together in silence for five minutes every day began to change the class dynamics.

They decided they wanted to have a calmer lunch period with a tablecloth, plates, and a "calmness manager" who would ring a bell if things got too noisy. It proved unnecessary to ring the bell even once, Premi told me, even on the very first day, and they want to continue this lunchtime practice for the rest of the term.

Then they began learning about the life of Martin Luther King. During their studies, they saw a photo of his followers practicing nonviolent resistance in a racially segregated diner. People were pouring ketchup on their heads, trying to provoke them.

Later Premi asked her class, "What can we share at the school assembly to honor Dr. King and his followers?"

"We could meditate!" was the first thing out of someone's mouth.

She asked them what they thought meditation had to do with Dr. King.

One student replied, "I feel calm when I meditate. Those people in the diner had to stay calm not to fight back."

Another said, "I want the world to have more peace and less hate, and when you are quiet you feel more peaceful."

"Love is inside you," said a third. "When I meditate and am quiet, I can see what's inside me."

Photo from Premi's blog at LiveInLaughter.com.

All this from second-graders who are meditating for five minutes a day. My friends, touching the silence that permeates everything is one of the fruits of meditation. Through that silence God can come to us, and in reaching out to embrace it, our lives will be transformed.

In divine stillness,
NAYASWAMI DEVI

56

Jan. 25, 2018

ANANDA SEVA

I am currently writing a book with the working title *Ananda Seva*, about the power of selfless service and how it can help dissolve the ego. Paramhansa Yogananda taught a path to liberation that combines both meditation and service. There is a wealth of resources to train and support aspirants in meditation: teachers, books, courses, meditation centers, websites, and apps. But even though most people spend much more time in outward activity than they do in meditation, very little is available that focuses on service as a spiritual practice. Even a little training in right attitudes and practices can turn our activity into a true spiritual path.

Can selfless service truly be a pathway to enlightenment? Swami Kriyananda told us this story: A young man came to an ashram to receive training from a guru. The guru assigned him the job of collecting wood for the cooking fires. Day after day, the youth continued his task, his whole focus on his job, unaware of the passage of time. One day, as he returned to the ashram, a tuft of his hair got caught between two sticks of wood, and he saw that his hair had turned completely white. He was stunned to realize that he was now an old man. A great sadness overwhelmed him. His whole life, he felt, had been wasted—he'd never even studied with his guru. Thinking these thoughts, he began to cry.

At that very moment the guru rushed out, and hastily stretched out his hand to catch the first tear as it fell. "Don't you know," he said lovingly, "that if the tears of such a great soul as you were to touch the ground, there would be famine in the land for seven years?" The guru then tapped him over the heart, and the man entered the highest state of samadhi. Such is the power of selfless service.

The book has an interesting origin. Five of us, all disciples of Paramhansa Yogananda and good friends, were sitting together in a restaurant in Delhi, India. We had spent the previous day together in Brindaban, where the Paramhansa Yogananda Public Charitable Trust is serving several thousand homeless or destitute widows. We were discussing the wonderful staff and how more than a third had recently learned meditation and become disciples of Yogananda.

Then a flash of insight came: Even though their day was spent serving, they had almost no formal training in service as a conscious spiritual practice. Service, rather than meditation, is by far the dominant part of most people's day; even the most dedicated meditator is likely to spend vastly more time in activity than in his meditation room. It became obvious that a book is needed to show why service is so important to our spiritual development, and how to do it properly.

As the four others continued their discussion, a powerful torrent of thoughts, ideas, and inspiration began to flow in me. Within fifteen minutes I had jotted down the basic concepts that compose the chapters of the book. Along with this strong flow of energy, there came a joyful sense of approval. It felt to me that the ideas were being blessed by Babaji himself.

Here are just a few of the key concepts:

> Ananda Seva (joy-filled service) can truly be a way of dissolving the ego.

> We should serve with a flow of God's love, both seeing those we serve as a form of the Divine and feeling that it is the Divine who is serving through us.

> The attitudes with which we serve are more important than the type of service.

Our primary goal in serving others is to uplift consciousness, both theirs and ours.

Ananda Seva should be done with high energy and magnetism using practical, efficient methods.

Our service should be rooted in a daily practice of meditation.

I am doing my best to follow these principles even in the writing of the book—to feel that it is the Divine Hand writing through me.

In service to the Divine,
NAYASWAMI JYOTISH

57
Feb. 1, 2018

WHEN *to* FIGHT BACK

There was a time in my life when it seemed as if circumstances were all conspiring to make me miserable. I would wake up every morning feeling pretty down, but in my mind there was still a spark of light that led me to think, "You've felt worse before. You can carry on today."

Finally one morning I woke up so downcast that even the spark of light was gone, and I thought, "We're breaking new ground here — I can't remember ever feeling this down before!"

Then I actually began to feel afraid, as though I was slipping down a dangerous slope without any ability to stop. At that point — I don't really know how it happened: maybe God's grace, Guru's blessings, or good karma — a fierce determination arose within me to fight back. I knew if I didn't take strong action right away to resist this downward pull that it would begin to gain the upper hand.

With determination (motivated more than a little by fear) I fought back with every weapon I had, using the teachings and techniques of Paramhansa Yogananda. I found an old Christmas card with the word *JOY* printed on it in embossed gold letters. Carefully I cut it out and taped it to a window in our room where I would see it throughout the day: a reminder of what I was fighting for. (Even now, many years later, I can still see those golden letters clearly in my mind's eye.)

On a physical level, I did the Energization Exercises with more dynamic awareness and went for regular vigorous walks. I found

Post this affirmation for joy in your home.

more ways to serve others and stay busy so that my energy wouldn't drop.

On a mental/emotional level, I acted as happy as I could around others (even if I wasn't feeling it inside); I didn't talk about negative subjects, but tried consciously to fill my mind with things that made me happy. I determined not to lower my guard even for a moment against the downward-pulling energy. And I returned to my room often to look at the golden letters of *JOY*.

On a spiritual level, I dug deeper in meditation, and was able to feel better during those times. I kept my mind constantly engaged inwardly singing Yogananda's chants, or mentally repeating the mantra, "Om Guru."

Then I found something Yoganandaji had written: "Life is a struggle for joy all along the way. May I fight to win the battle on the very spot where I now am." His words resonated deep in my heart and invigorated my efforts to fight back. Finally the pickaxe of my determination dug into the slippery slope of unhappiness, and I was able to stop my fall.

Then began the upward ascent. Each day I felt a bit lighter and freer from dark moods. Finally the day dawned when I burst onto new ground once again, but this time a different landscape awaited me. A sense of joy unlike anything I had experienced before began to fill me. It stayed with me for many months; then it slowly diminished, though not completely. The memory of that

experience has remained, ever a reminder to me of what to strive for.

There are many lessons from this experience, on which I have drawn over the years:

1. Recognize when it's time to fight back, and swing into action.
2. Exert unwavering determination — it wins out in the end.
3. Trust that divine guides are always with us to protect and guide us through our trials.
4. The resolution of every test brings greater joy.

When tests come to you, friend, remember to summon up courage and determination to win the battle on the very spot on which you stand.

In loving friendship,
NAYASWAMI DEVI

58
Feb. 8, 2018

WE NEED NEW SELF-DEFINITIONS

A friend recently sent us an article by the head of Mercedes Benz, talking about some of the disruptive changes that are coming due to the combination of AI (artificial intelligence) and robotics. For instance, we are on the cusp of self-driving vehicles, which is exciting news for most people, but an existential threat to automakers and truck drivers. But this is just the tip of the iceberg. One of the fastest-developing, and potentially most disruptive, changes is a type of artificial intelligence, called neural networks, that mimics the way the brain learns.

Two years ago a computer was finally able to beat the world champion at a complex game called "Go." Then came neural networks which, rather than being carefully programmed, are simply given a goal and instructed to figure out a strategy by trial and error. Each time it plays a game, it evolves according to what works and what doesn't. The game changer is in the phrase "each time," because it can play thousands of games each hour. Such a program recently taught itself to beat the top ten Go players simultaneously, which doesn't sound too impressive until you hear that,

Photo by NASA.gov.

Paramhansa Yogananda and Rajarshi Janakananda.

starting from scratch, it figured out how to do this in just three days.

AI is already better than humans at hundreds of tasks such as pattern recognition, facial identification, reading medical tests, doing taxes, and driving. Futurists say that by 2025, artificial intelligence and robots will replace virtually all repetitive work and 25% of people may lose their jobs. By 2035 most professions will be gone, with as many as 50% out of work. By 2050 there will be very few of our present jobs left for humans. So, where does this all lead?

It will mean that people need to develop a new bundle of self-definitions, which is one way Swami Kriyananda described the ego. Our new self-identity can no longer depend on occupation, or income level, or the status in society that those represent. We will need to self-define more according to the qualities of our higher chakras, such as love, kindness, caring, and joy.

Finally, it means that we will need to tune in more deeply to God and His eternal qualities. As strangers in a strange new land, we will need to let His whispers guide us through the landscape. The Masters know all of this, of course. Here are some fascinating excerpts from a letter that Paramhansa Yogananda wrote to his most advanced disciple, Rajarshi Janakananda, that give us a glimpse into a world of higher realities:

> I have been doing a million things; and I compared my divine state with work and I found this truth: Very few of us know how to differentiate between the duties created by us and the duties assigned to us by God. Most think of their own desire-created duties as divine duties. Human desire-created duties bind and cause reincarnation. . . .

First find what the divine duties are, then use your own ambition to accomplish them, asking God all the time to guide your creative effort and will to perform them as the Divine wishes.

Oh, such joy! I don't feel any sensations making any permanent impression in me. The ordinary man walks, sleeps, works, earns. I find I am settled in Bliss. I am always in Bliss, ever watching the states of the body and mind when they are awake or asleep or dreaming. Last night I ate, and when I finished I didn't know I had eaten. All I knew was Bliss Eternal and Light ever spreading. Even now *Aum* is bounding over my head, tying it with the starry firmament. It is all very strange, all very secret. By meditation He makes the servant sit on the throne. Oh, this secret kingdom is yours and mine, beloved one. There is our permanent ashram, an astral hermitage, a bliss cavern.

Now, that is a future worth living for.

In divine friendship,
NAYASWAMI JYOTISH

The HAPPINESS THIEVES

Yale University recently offered a course that's proved to be the most popular one ever given there. The topic was "Happiness." One-quarter of the student body—twelve hundred undergraduates—enrolled, requiring the largest auditorium on campus for the classes.

Why so much interest? One student said, "In reality, a lot of us are anxious, stressed, unhappy, and numb." Unfortunately, this statement is not limited to Yale undergrads. The complexity and accelerating pace of life, heightened competition, and increasing human isolation are robbing us of peace of mind. As a result, people find themselves desperate to find that most elusive quality in life: happiness.

Paramhansa Yogananda has written about what he called the "happiness thieves"—patterns of behavior that steal our joy. Let's look at a few of these "thieves," and how we can enlist our "Soul Patrols" to drive them away.

Thief #1: Negative Habits. When we repeatedly express qualities like anger, self-interest, or laziness, they become hardwired in our brain. The longer these habits are allowed to go unchecked, the more entrenched they become. We can, however, call on our Soul Patrol of "Freedom from Bad Habits" to combat them with energy and will power. By expressing their opposites—kindness, generosity, or dynamic activity—we begin to establish new neural pathways that enable us to live more joyfully.

Thief #2: Speaking Negatively About Others. Everything and everyone in this world is a mixture of good and bad qualities. That is the nature of duality. If you find that you tend regularly to talk about what's *wrong* with others, realize that this is diminishing your own happiness. Call on the Soul Patrol of "Seeing the Highest in All," and begin to speak about what's *right* about them. You'll find a shift in your perspective, like a shaft of light illumining your mind, that will bring a sense of freedom and joy.

Thief #3: Worrying. If you're often in a state of anxiety about what might happen in the future, call on the Soul Patrol of "Determined Peace of Mind." Yoganandaji has written, "Happiness comes, not by helplessly wishing for it, but by thinking and living it in all circumstances. No matter what you are doing, keep the undercurrent of happiness flowing beneath the sands of your thoughts and the rocky soil of trials."

I'll close with a true story told to us by a dear friend in India. He and his family are direct disciples of the great woman saint, Anandamayi Ma, who often stayed with them in their home.

Once when our friend was sixteen, he contracted dysentery. His condition worsened, and eventually he had to be hospitalized. Nothing the medical staff did seemed to help; his pain and weakness increased daily. Finally the doctors told him and his family that there was nothing more they could do: He would not survive.

Photo from www.AnandamayiMa.org.

Our friend lay in bed too weak to move, overwhelmed by pain, and with tears falling down his cheeks. At that moment, Anandamayi Ma entered his hospital room.

"Son," she said, "I can't help you if you remain so unhappy. You need to stop crying and smile for me."

Feebly he replied, "Ma, how can I smile now?"

"Try," she told him.

Summoning up what little strength he had left, he forced himself to stop crying, and wanly smiled at her. Immediately she began to rub his body with her hands, and he felt energy and healing flowing into him. To everyone's amazement, in a few days he returned to full health.

To draw divine grace that is the source of true, lasting happiness, we need to do our part. Find the strength to reach out for happiness, and God will do the rest. Then the happiness thieves will flee, never to return.

With joy,
NAYASWAMI DEVI

60
Feb. 22, 2018

The PILLARS of the PATH

Here at Ananda Village we are in the midst of our annual Inner Renewal Week. Each year we have two weeks of classes, one held in August and the other in February, which act as anchors, keeping the ship of our lives from drifting out to sea on the tides of spiritual apathy.

Swami Kriyananda suggested that Ananda members have the goal of becoming a jivan mukta in this lifetime. This lofty ambition requires that the soul release itself from its dream of ego, and during this week we are looking at how to accomplish this through the three pillars of our path: sadhana, seva, and attunement.

We started the classes with this story: Some years ago Devi and I were with Swamiji discussing how difficult it seemed to become a jivan mukta, and how inadequate we felt toward the task. He was at breakfast and paused in the middle of a bite, the fork halfway to his mouth. He summed up the entire divine search with these few words: "The whole purpose of the spiritual path is to overcome the delusion of ego. This is done by longer, deeper meditation, and by seeing God as the Doer in everything." Then he finished his bite. He might have added the third pillar, attunement to the guru, which at other times he said was the most important factor of all.

Sadhana helps the soul release itself from the delusion that it is merely this body and personality. Our spiritual practices help us achieve this by reversing, generally through meditation techniques, the flow of life-force from its usual downward and outward direction. When the prana flows outward through the senses, we are subject to the delusion that fulfillment can be found outside our Self. Kriya Yoga is the most effective and scientific way to withdraw the life-force back through our own central nervous system, first bringing it to the spiritual eye, and then eventually releasing our consciousness from the body altogether. In addition to deep meditation, any act, thought, desire, or habit that helps dissolve the ego can be considered as sadhana.

Seva is the way the soul expresses love, friendship, and compassion toward others. Selfless service is a true pathway to liberation if we can act with the awareness that, in essence, all activity is God serving God. When our attitudes and habits are aligned toward this end, our life becomes a beautiful expression of God's love in action.

Attunement with the guru is the third pillar. Our main obstacle is the multitude of desires and habits that impel our consciousness outward. By attuning our mind to that of someone who is already free, we attract his consciousness and, more importantly, his blessing. Grace radiating from God and Guru does seventy-five percent of the work for us. Our twenty-five percent is accomplished mainly through willing, joyful, disciplined cooperation with that grace.

If we can get these three pillars right, we will be well on our way to becoming a jivan mukta. If you're interested, you can find the full recordings of the classes at joyiswith.in/5.

In joy,
NAYASWAMI JYOTISH

"The ART of FOLLOWING": An ALLEGORY

Here is a story that came to me for our class on attunement during Inner Renewal Week.

A teacher gives each of his students a map and tells them, "This map leads to a great treasure. Each of your maps is different, but they'll all lead you to the same prize."

Then he adds, "But follow only the one I've given you. Don't look at anyone else's map."

With eager anticipation, they set out as a group on their journey.

At first the way is easy, along a familiar road. They talk and laugh along the way, enjoying the fellowship and the promise of treasure.

After a while, some of the students grow bored with the unvarying landscape, and decide to take what looks like a shortcut. Some of these are never seen again. After some time the others are observed returning, looking tired and disappointed. These wanderers find that they must return to the point where they departed from their map.

"Master with the Children," by Nayaswami Jyotish.

Still another group become impatient with the plodding route given to them and think, "It looks like my neighbor has a better, easier path. I'll take a peek at his map and follow that." But when they begin to follow the other's way, it leads them to a dead end, or to the precipice of a high cliff. They, too, must retrace their steps back to where they diverged.

But there is a third group who think, "I will follow the path that my teacher gave me, although it seems slow and the landscape unchanging."

The impatient ones looking for a quicker way begin to taunt them: "Can't you think for yourself? Our teacher doesn't even have a GPS! His ways are antiquated!"

"Never mind," the patient ones reply. "I will follow the way given to me. Our teacher has the best GPS — '**G**od's **P**ole**S**tar.'"

As the students continue toward the treasure, the lines on their map become fainter, until they are almost invisible. The countryside is now unfamiliar and strange. They grow uneasy.

Some say, "I've come so far, but I don't know how to proceed. I'll stay here, and perhaps in time guidance will come."

Others ask directions from strangers they meet along the road, and depart back to familiar territory.

But a small group inwardly call to their teacher, "I have made you polestar of my life. Though my way is dark, and my stars are gone, let me find my way through your mercy." The lines on their map mysteriously begin to reappear, and now are traced in gold.

Finally, as this handful of students grow closer to the end of their quest, a dark cloud envelops them. To their shock, their map is now completely blank!

"Teacher," they cry in distress, "I am lost and afraid. Why have you abandoned me so close to the treasure?"

In the darkness they hear his voice say, "To those who think me near, I will be near. Go within and feel my guidance."

In inner stillness, the students see a beautiful golden light within their forehead. In it appears a radiant blue field with a silvery-white star in the middle, beckoning them forward.

They realize that this last stage of their journey isn't traveled by outer pathways, but through the inner landscape of consciousness. The faithful few allow their map to fall from their hands, and hear their teacher's voice saying, "Surrender to me all that you are, or know, or have."

With devotion and trust, they surrender completely, and realize that the treasure they were seeking was never outside of them. It was always within, waiting for that moment of total self-offering to their teacher, their divine friend, their guru.

Hand in hand, guru and disciple move forward through the silvery star to the inner treasure they were seeking: their eternal home in the kingdom of God.

In divine friendship,
NAYASWAMI DEVI

AMAZING DAY, AMAZING GRACE

I experienced an amazing day when I was young, and it still echoes through the corridors of my memory. I was around six years old, living in a small town in northern Iowa. Our home sat across the street from a large park in a hilly part of town, and my youth was spent playing and exploring among its trees, ponds, and grass. Those images, imprinted on my young mind, still form the "magic cloth" of the tapestry in some of my dreams.

A fairylike day dawned in the depths of winter. The ground was covered with snow, which was not unusual, since snow normally arrived in the late fall. Then it covered the ground until those magical days of spring when, as the poet e. e. cummings wrote, "The world is mud-luscious and puddle-wonderful."

This day was different. Something strange and unusual had happened during the night, perhaps a warming spell followed by a deep freeze. The result was magical for a budding young adventurer like me: There was a thin crust of frozen ice covering the whole snowy landscape. It sparkled in the

"First Day of Spring," by Nayaswami Jyotish.

morning light like a trillion diamonds, but beauty was the least of its wonders.

I could walk on it, although I had to be careful—if I jumped or ran, I broke through the crust. But if I treaded lightly, I was supported. And it was ice-rink slippery, fun for sliding. We occasionally visited frozen ponds and found them diverting for a few minutes, but this was different. This was the whole terrain. And it wasn't flat and boring: It had hills!

My friends and I quickly figured out that we could slide down the hills on sheets of cardboard. These were not "sissified" slopes suitable for sleds and toddlers. There were trees to be avoided. Or not. We spent a whole morning sliding down, slogging back up, and launching ourselves into the danger once again. Finally, with my body bruised and my wonder sated, I headed home for a hot lunch, bubbling over with tales of my adventure.

I think this incident has lingered in my mind because there were so many lessons in it. First, it took several positive traits to take advantage of this opportunity: enthusiasm, courage, determination—a spirit of adventuresomeness. But another spiritual message comes to mind:

Our whole world is covered by a thin crust of grace, beautiful and delicate. If we are too heavy with worry, doubt, and cynicism, the fragile grace can't support us. If we trod through life with anger, negativity, or indifference, we break through the delicate covering and lose all sense of the world's beauty and wonder. But if we glide lightly over whatever befalls us, we can experience life's wonder and joy.

Far too often as we grow up, we grow grim. We learn to fear and reject the slippery slopes of life, which God gives us for our "education and entertainment." And we grow too sophisticated and prideful to be content with a simple piece of cardboard or a simple life.

When Swami Kriyananda was a new disciple, Paramhansa Yogananda told him that he was too serious. "You need to become more childlike," he said, and quoted the saying of Jesus, "Suffer little children to come unto me, and forbid them not: for of such is the kingdom of God."

Let's recall those magical days of childhood that linger still in our memories. Better yet, let's become childlike once again, and play on God's hills and valleys.

In childlike joy,
NAYASWAMI JYOTISH

63
March 15, 2018

WHAT IS THIS LIFE?

Whenever we get a chance to visit Hawaii, we're awed by the power of life force, or *prana*, that permeates everything here. It's amazing to see the variety of plants that grow to a height of maybe four or five inches on the mainland, but that here in Hawaii reach six to ten feet with flowers and leaves radiant with life and color.

The understanding and use of *prana* is one of the keynotes of Paramhansa Yogananda's teachings: in the Energization Exercises, magnetized prayers and affirmations, and Kriya Yoga. When Yoganandaji was on his hugely successful lecture tours in America, he would often address crowded auditoriums, saying, "There is enough energy in one gram of flesh [here he would pinch his arm to illustrate] to keep the city of Chicago supplied with electricity for a week!"

The trick is to become aware of this life force, which is within and around us everywhere, and direct it to where it's needed.

Recently while a friend of mine from Italy was traveling in India, she slipped and broke a bone in her ankle. The doctor applied a below-the-knee cast, and told her

A photo I took in Hawaii.

she shouldn't put any weight on it or travel for several weeks. Being a lifelong practitioner of Yoganandaji's teaching, she spent her "house arrest" in a hotel room, daily sending energy to the broken bone, and visualizing it whole again.

After three weeks, the doctor was amazed when she looked at the new x-rays, and said, "Remarkable healing." She removed the cumbersome, heavy cast, and gave her a light air cast. Our friend will soon be on the road again.

But this life force can be used for more than just healing broken bones, because *prana* is also conscious. The parts of our life that are broken in other ways—unresolved emotions, past hurts, karmic blocks with people, patterns of mental resistance—all can be healed by directed life force.

First we need to become sensitively aware of where the "break" in the energy flow is, and then channel *prana* there. Without needing to analyze exactly why or how the problem arose psychologically, we can send the consciously-aware life force to untangle our emotional knots and make us whole again. The key is to be ready to let go of the past, and to allow the flow of subtle energy to heal us.

Ultimately, for those seeking spiritual freedom, we can direct this *prana* in meditation, sending it to higher centers of awareness. When we do this repeatedly through regular practice, our consciousness becomes filled with energy and expands to feel its oneness with a greater reality.

Like the little plants that grow to be huge when bathed in Hawaii's *prana*, we can become heightened expressions of ourselves. Once we know how to work with this divine life force, we can use it to unlock our own potential—physically, mentally, and spiritually—and begin to realize who and what we really are.

As Yoganandaji once said, "What is this life flowing in my veins? Could it be other than divine?"

With joy in this life,
NAYASWAMI DEVI

A PLACE of REFUGE

Last week, here on the island of Hawaii, we visited an interesting historical site called "The Place of Refuge." The old Hawaiian culture was hierarchical, with the king at the top, the warriors and artisans beneath him, and then, at the lowest level, the vast majority—those who fished and worked the land. There were many laws concerning what was "kapu," or forbidden, and someone breaking one of these rules could easily receive a death sentence. However, one could avoid certain death by fleeing to a temple at "The Place of Refuge," where the offender would be absolved by a priest and freed to leave.

This may be a portrayal of ancient Hawaii, but it is really the story of mankind. Throughout recorded history, including modern times, we see variations of these same forces at play. The desire for power and status is one of the strongest of all the drives of ego. It is expressed by animals establishing a "pecking order," as well as by playground bullies and greedy tyrants. Lurking behind many of today's headlines you can see power struggles that are not very different from ancient times. The difference is that, in today's world, there are few "Places of Refuge."

Puʻuhonua o Hōnaunau National Historical Park.

Why? Because the outer world is always an expression of inner consciousness. In these restless times, if we have no place

Create a place of refuge for everyone and everything.

of refuge within, we will find none without. People often spend a fortune and a lifetime vainly looking for security in an unsafe world. Unfortunately, they rarely find it in the dream of maya, for as Shakespeare said, life is only a tale "filled with sound and fury signifying nothing."

Can a place of refuge be found anywhere? Yes, but nowhere on the face of the earth. It is in your heart when it is filled with devotion, and in the light at your spiritual eye.

Here is the tricky part for most people: In the realm of consciousness, we are both the condemning king and the absolving priest. God does not condemn us, nor does the guru. They are pure love, pure friendship. We condemn ourselves by transgressing against the "kapu" areas of the law of karma.

In order to move on, we need to start by absolving ourselves of our ignorance. If you find it hard to accept yourself with all your kinks and blemishes, start by accepting and loving others. Begin with those closest to you: your family, friends, and coworkers. When you create a place of refuge for one person, you automatically create the same space for yourself. If you need more safety and security, then widen your circle of acceptance to everyone around you. If that still is not enough, if you still don't feel an unshakable security, then create a place of refuge for everyone and everything. Judge no one, love everyone.

Then, perhaps for the first time ever, you'll find an inner kingdom of peace in the midst of your own paradise island.

In love and joy,
NAYASWAMI JYOTISH

65
March 29, 2018

WHOM ARE YOU TRYING *to* PLEASE?

Early in their time together, Paramhansa Yogananda instructed his direct disciple, Swami Kriyananda, that his work in this lifetime would be lecturing, editing, and writing. When I met Swamiji in 1969, he was constantly engaged in these three activities, as well as in the Herculean task of launching the spiritual communities movement through Ananda.

His was not a typical yogi's life of non-involvement, but one that demanded much of his physical, mental, and spiritual strength. Yet no matter how much energy traveling, lecturing, or other responsibilities required of him, he produced a steady stream of inspiring, beautifully written books.

I remember once discussing with him a writing project that he wanted me to undertake. Unsure of myself, I said to him, "Swamiji, I'm not a very good writer." Not allowing me any room for excuses, he replied simply, "Then you'd better roll up your sleeves and get to work."

Observing his life was always a powerful teaching. He was an accomplished writer from his early years, but nevertheless he worked incredibly hard at it. "Sometimes," he told us, "I'll edit a new chapter fifty times before I'm totally satisfied with it."

Once he shared with us a story about writing that he said was a joke on him. He'd received a letter from someone who praised him for his clear, inspiring writing style. The next day, as he began working on the book at hand, he thought to himself, "I'd better

do a good job today. I don't want to disappoint my public."

But as he tried to write, he couldn't get into his usual creative flow. Realizing that he was writing to please "his public," he then laughed, put this thought out of his mind, and started all over again. This time he concentrated on attunement with his guru and the points he wanted to make, and he quickly "got his groove" back.

Swamiji once said that working to win the approval or recognition of others is slavery, whereas working to please only God is freedom.

Overcoming the need for people's praise is a big challenge for all of us. A friend of mine recently wrote for advice about how to rise above this need, and to serve more with the thought of pleasing God. Here are some suggestions I gave her:

> 1. If someone praises your service, remember that any good thing we do flows through us from God. Mentally thank God for helping whoever has thanked you.

> 2. In working with a team, make sure that everyone shares in the credit for what is done, and take as little of it for yourself as possible.

> 3. In meditation at night, consciously offer to God everything you've done that day, and then release it.

> 4. Repeat regularly these words of Yoganandaji: "Beloved Father, I realize that praise does not make me better, nor blame worse. I am what I am before my conscience and Thee. I shall travel on, doing good to all and seeking ever to please Thee, for thus shall I find my only true happiness."

In all that you do—even the humblest task—consciously seek to please only our Heavenly Father/Divine Mother. Their approval earns us the lasting joy of ego-transcendence.

In loving friendship,
NAYASWAMI DEVI

66
April 5, 2018

COOPERATING *with* GRACE

As I write this, we're in India for two weeks on an unexpected trip. A series of completely unforeseen events has provided the potential for a wonderful new project. Working with one of India's premiere leaders in education, our small team is creating a vision and feasibility study for a world-class Institute of Leadership based on Paramhansa Yogananda's principles of higher consciousness. If it comes into manifestation, it will be the fulfillment of a dream of Swamiji's, and a vehicle for the upliftment of world consciousness. The project is in such an early phase, with clarity just starting to emerge, that it's too early to share any more details at this time.

I want to write about another subject related to this unexpected trip—cooperating with divine grace. Occasionally an opportunity presents itself that may be inconvenient for our existing schedule. When this happens, and previously laid-out plans have to be cast aside, in the dark corners of my mind I wonder if God is paying the close attention to my calendar that I think it deserves.

So, how should we act when the Divine sends an opportu-

"God's Grace," by Nayaswami Jyotish.

nity, or a test, that requires some sacrifice on our part? We would do well to follow the counsel of Sister Gyanamata, Master's most advanced woman disciple. Her advice was to "Say 'yes,' and make it snappy."

When Master was still a young man, he founded a school for boys in Ranchi, India. One morning, as he was meditating in a tiny storeroom (the only place where he could find a little privacy), he had a vision and heard a clear call to go to America. In spite of his heavy responsibilities, he left the school and began making arrangements for his trip to the West that same afternoon.

Similarly, in 2003 Swami Kriyananda received an email from a devotee in India saying that Master's work there needed more energy. To us, it was a simple letter, but to Swamiji it was a call from the Divine. Within two weeks, at the tender age of seventy-seven, he had moved to India to start Ananda's work here. The result of his willingness to follow the divine call is that hundreds of thousands of people are being helped through Yogananda's teachings.

There are many more stories with this same theme: A call is heard, and acted upon; divine grace acts like a wind at your back, and miracles happen. There are also countless times when God's call is not answered, but we never hear of those stories. His seeds fall upon barren ground, and no flowers grow.

We need to prepare the garden of our hearts by constantly doing our best to align our individual will to the divine will. The day will come when God asks something of us, when He is trying to plant a seed. It may not always be convenient to say yes, but it is the surest path to liberation. Remember, *everything* that comes to us is a gift of love from Divine Mother. Whether pleasant or unpleasant, convenient or inconvenient, it is given with love and, if accepted gratefully, will lead to freedom.

I can attest, from my own experience, that great joy comes when we learn to "say 'yes,' and make it snappy."

In joyful acceptance,
NAYASWAMI JYOTISH

67
April 12, 2018

EXPRESS YOUR SELF!

As we entered the art room and took in the paint-splattered tables and small plastic chairs, we felt as if we were back in grade school. We took our seats, and saw at each place a row of paint jars containing a variety of colors; large, flat brushes; and a medium-sized piece of white art paper.

The afternoon was part of a women's retreat that included group meditations, hatha yoga sessions, nature walks, and guided group discussions. Today we were having an art workshop led by one of the resident artists at Ananda Village.

Our instructor was a joyful, free spirit who told us, "Paint whatever comes to mind." Suddenly everyone froze.

Woeful cries of "I'm not creative," "I'm a terrible painter," "I was awful in art class" filled the air.

But our instructor had heard all this before. She suggested, "Everyone look at the different colors in the jars in front of you, and then close your eyes and see which color fills your mind. Now dip the brush in that jar, and move it across your paper."

To our delight, each of us was able to produce a large swath of bright color on the blank white paper. The instructor guided us in the next step: "Now feel what colors or shapes you would like to add." At first tentatively, and then with more gusto, each one began painting whatever came to mind.

After we finished our initial attempts, and had broken down some of the inner resistances, we moved away from the tables and began painting on large pieces of paper taped to the wall.

Little by little, as everyone was able to relax, we put more energy into our painting, and began to enjoy ourselves. Our original self-critical and self-limiting thoughts of "I can't" or "I'm no good at this" melted away in the enjoyment of blending colors and creating images.

Swami Kriyananda visits the Ananda preschool.

Did any of us create a masterpiece? Admittedly no. Did many of us produce surprisingly nice paintings? Assuredly so. But did all of us have a great time filled with the freedom and joy of self-expression? Absolutely yes.

Paramhansa Yogananda taught the importance of creativity and a positive flow of energy for spiritual development. He challenged his students to try every day to do something in a new way they hadn't tried before.

Whether it's rearranging the furniture in our home, planning a project with our colleagues at work, relaxing with our family, or practicing techniques of meditation, if we apply creativity and self-expression to our activities we can discover the joy of feeling God's creative power flowing through us.

God is, after all, the consummate artist. Every wayside flower, each fallen leaf, the smile on a baby's face—everything from the tiniest pebble to the greatest Himalayan peak—is an expression of His creativity. This power lies also within each one of us, and will flow freely once we rise above self-criticism and limitation—the "no-saying" principle.

Yoganandaji offered this "Sacred Invitation" to us all:

> Come out of your closed chamber of limitation. Breathe in the fresh air of vital thoughts. Exhale poisonous thoughts of discouragement, discontentment, and hopelessness. . . . Take long mental walks on the path

of self-confidence. Feast unstintingly on creative thinking within yourself and others.

You are all gods, if you only knew it. You must look within. Behind the wave of your consciousness is the sea of God's presence. Claim your Divine Birthright. Awake, and you shall see the glory of God.

With freedom of spirit,
NAYASWAMI DEVI

The POWER of DIVINE PLACES

We were sitting with two dear friends at a retreat house in the foothills of the Himalayas, where we take a yearly seclusion. One of them asked me if I felt a special power here and if my meditations were any deeper. I told her that for me personally, this is one of the two most sacred places on earth. The other is the Moksha Mandir at Ananda Village, where Swami Kriyananda's body rests. Both are places wholly dedicated to prayer and meditation, with no other vibrations mixed in. As a result, each has a special purity, and great spiritual magnetism.

The rainbow ring we saw around the sun.

This is only a brief visit, two days squeezed out of an intensely busy schedule. We came to India to help with the formation of an Institute of Leadership and Service, based on the spiritual principles taught by Paramhansa Yogananda. Although our daily meetings with a small team of consultants have gone amazingly well, we still wanted to ask for the guidance and blessings of God, our gurus, and Swami Kriyananda.

Certain places, often pilgrimage spots, act as powerful spiritual amplifiers, and devotees go to great lengths to visit them and bask in their holy ambiance. It is especially helpful to visit such places when facing an important task or juncture in one's life. A case in point is an episode Yogananda related in his *Autobiography of a*

Nanda Devi peeking out for us in blessing.

Yogi, in the chapter "The Heart of a Stone Image." His eldest sister, Roma, had asked him to intercede with her materialistic husband. Master wrote: "An inspiration seized me. 'Tomorrow,' I said, 'I am going to the Dakshineswar temple. Please come with me, and persuade your husband to accompany us. I feel that in the vibrations of that holy place, Divine Mother will touch his heart.'" And so She did.

We came on this retreat hoping that Divine Mother would touch our hearts also. The house where we're staying is in an area where the Pandavas lived in ancient times; Babaji feels particularly close here. We weren't really expecting any outward sign of blessing, but it is nice when it comes of itself. Many times on Swami Kriyananda's birthday, a rainbow had appeared in a clear blue sky in what is called a "glory." His Ananda friends have always associated that phenomenon with God's blessing upon him. Yesterday, in the late afternoon, in a nearly clear sky, there appeared a rainbow ring around the sun. It was something none of us had ever seen before, and we felt as if Swamiji had somehow arranged it for us.

Now, on this morning of our last day here, another sign of blessing was given us. The distant mountains seem to stand guard over the house. Especially beautiful is Nanda Devi, perhaps the most sacred of all the Himalayan peaks. Legend says that you cannot demand to see her, that she will only reveal herself to you if it be her wish. For the last two days she had not chosen to do so, but on this final morning she peeked out above the clouds. It felt like Divine Mother had heard our earnest prayers, and wanted to make sure we knew that we had Her blessings on this sacred project.

In joy,
NAYASWAMI JYOTISH

BEAUTY *and* GRACE

Imagine seventeen thousand tulips in an amazing variety of shapes, colors, and sizes, all blooming amidst the vast vistas of the Sierra Nevada mountains of California. April is the time for "Springtime at Ananda," the annual tulip festival at Crystal Hermitage Gardens, and thousands of viewers come from throughout the state to enjoy the superlative beauty.

You are welcome here. Enjoy the beauty, and feel a touch of God's joy in your heart.

These gardens have a special magic that attracts and uplifts people. The sensitive blending of colors and the imaginative landscaping are sublime. And the flowers themselves seem to understand that they are serving as channels of God's blessings to all who come. In every imaginable hue, the radiant blossoms nod gently in the breeze as if to say, "You are welcome here. Enjoy the beauty, and feel a touch of God's joy in your heart."

Last Saturday as we walked through the gardens, what struck us even more than the variety of flowers was the variety of people who had come. The diversity of religions, races, and nationalities enjoying the beautiful natural display was wonderful to see.

Visitors to these gardens come year after year, bringing their children, parents, and friends. Last weekend one family especially caught my eye, a multigenerational Hispanic family: bright-eyed, energetic children; patient, slower-moving grandparents; and bustling, organizing parents all happily gathered together to enjoy a picnic in this haven of peace and beauty.

The place they chose to eat was an outdoor patio table—a table at which Swami Kriyananda would often sit to rest during his afternoon walks through the garden. So many memories of happy, precious moments came flooding back to me of times spent with Swamiji at this table.

Thinking of the Hispanic families in America now living in fear of being deported and separated, my heart was filled with joy seeing their happy faces. Inwardly I thought, "Swamiji, you've created a little oasis of peace for this family at your table." And in response I felt his smile in my heart.

These gardens are a microcosm of the natural beauty which shines equally on everyone. Rain, sun, wind, clouds, trees, and flowers—all of nature—are expressions of God's love and grace shining without boundaries on all His children. They are messengers to awaken us to our unity with all people, all life, and, ultimately, with God.

For even the beauty of the Hermitage Gardens is only a dim reflection of the divine garden of God's kingdom. As Paramhansa Yogananda wrote in his *Whispers from Eternity*:

> O Flower of Fragrance! Send us the scent of love, to inspire us always in our search for Thee with longing to climb ever higher into the stratosphere of divine realization. May dreams of Thy perfect garden, far above all space and time—but near to us always, in our hearts!—speed our souls' journey and quench our thirst in Thee.

May we all find that sacred, hidden garden of divine beauty within.

Your friend in God,
NAYASWAMI DEVI

70
May 3, 2018

SELF-CONTROL

We heard a good joke recently. A man and his young grandson are shopping in a supermarket. The little boy is fussing and whining, wanting to leave.

The grandfather says, "Be patient, William. We only have two more items to get and then we can go."

A few moments later, the grandson is again complaining, and the grandfather says, "Just one last item to find, and then we can go, William."

Finally they are in the checkout line, and the boy is still acting out and making a scene. The grandfather says, "We're almost done, William. We just have to pay, and then we can go to the car."

As they're leaving, a woman comes up to the man and says, "I have been observing how patient you are with your grandson William. I want to congratulate you on your kindness."

The man replies, "Thank you, madam, but you misunderstand. *I* am William, my grandson's name is Harry."

I've told this joke a few times, and it always gets a laugh. It's such a common situation that it resonates with everyone. But, as with many jokes, there is a deeper side to it.

We all find ourselves in situations that are unpleasant, but from which there is no easy escape. We can learn from William how to handle such times. If we let frustration get the upper hand, it will lead to anger, which will then lead to conflict. It is a self-reinforcing negative cycle experienced by both individuals and nations.

Or, we can break the cycle by affirming a positive quality that neutralizes the negative energy. Here, William is using a sort of simple affirmation, a "Be patient" mantra. Repeatedly Paramhansa Yogananda talked about the importance of positivity on the spiritual path. There are three simple steps to greater self-control:

1. Control the reactive process. Try to give yourself a little time, even a few seconds, before you respond. Those few seconds give you the space to act rather than *react*. Take a few deep breaths. Count to ten. Repeat a simple affirmation. Stretch your spine. Do anything to gain the space you need, and you will find it much easier not to get drawn into an adverse response, which would sustain a negative cycle.

2. Neutralize the negative force coming toward you with its positive opposite. The boy was impatient, so the grandfather affirmed patience. Affirmations work because the world is made up of opposing polarities. A positive thought creates a positive flow of energy in the neural circuits of the brain, which creates a positive magnetism, or force field. The opposite is, of course, also true, and most of the time people simply react, reinforcing the negative magnetism, which leads to conflict.

3. Communicate your positive response. The grandfather didn't ignore the boy, he reassured him. When faced with negativity, be sure to let the other person know that you have heard them. Otherwise they will get angrier and shout louder just to be sure they have your attention.

The central point here is that trying to make the world conform to your wishes will only lead to frustration—it is hard enough to control our own behavior. But that, my friends, is the task given to each of us. Self-control is the fast lane to Self-realization.

In patient joy,
NAYASWAMI JYOTISH

FIVE STEPS to SELF-REALIZATION

As plants grow toward the sun's light, so too do our souls reach up toward the light of God. At first our inner growth may seem slow and hesitant, but gradually, as the yearning in our heart grows stronger, our movement towards the light gains momentum. Eventually, and this is true for everyone, the magnetism of God's presence within us becomes such a powerful force that we fairly rush to embrace it.

"To the Mountaintop," by Nayaswami Jyotish.

Recently I began thinking about various phases on the spiritual path that, though challenging, are all necessary to reach the journey's end: Self-realization. Here are some of the steps we take as we move from the little "self" to the big "Self."

1. Self-Righteousness. Often when we begin our journey we can get a little full of ourselves, and entertain thoughts like: "I'm practicing yoga and meditation, so I'm different, perhaps even a bit better than most people—more insightful, more aware." This attitude is self-defeating, because it reinforces our sense of separation from others. True spiritual growth should awaken within us a sense of kinship with others, based on the understanding that all people—from the best to the worst—are parts of our own self.

2. Self-Honesty. Eventually, as we continue on the spiritual path and are confronted with karma's inevitable tests, awareness dawns that maybe we aren't quite so "elevated" as we may once have thought. Gradually we awaken from complacency to the understanding that we have a lot of work to do on ourselves. We realize that our ego has misled us into imagining the source of our problems to be outside of us, rather than within our own consciousness.

And so we begin to look within and see what attitudes and behaviors need to be changed—and changed now! As we clear the field of our consciousness with the plow of self-honesty, we begin to feel a sense of purpose which leads us to the next step:

3. Self-Acceptance. In many ways this is the most important step on our journey. It's the starting point from which we can begin to work positively with the specific karmic challenges that we face. Self-acceptance enables us to stand on the firm ground of the reality of who we are right now. From that point, we can see where we want and need to go next, and how to get there. Self-acceptance also leads to the important step of:

4. Self-Forgetfulness. Self-forgetfulness is the steppingstone to inner freedom and joy. In the grand scheme of things, none of us is really all that important. Once a college friend of Swami Kriyananda's was complaining to his mother that no one appreciated his true worth. She gave him a good answer, though a tough one to hear: "Son, you're actually not important enough for people to spend a lot of time considering you, one way or the other."

This is true for all of us, and is actually cause not for lamenting but rejoicing. To lose oneself in the contemplation of the vast beauties of nature, or in the profound wisdom of a sage, or the sweetness of a mother tending her baby, or the unconditional love of God is to take a big spiritual step forward. In fact, self-forgetfulness is such an advanced stage of spiritual development that it leads us to the final step on the journey:

5. Self-Realization. Paramhansa Yogananda said, "When this 'I' shall die, then shall I know who am I." Finding God is not entering uncharted territory: It is a journey that has been made by dedicated men and women down through the ages. It is your journey, it is mine. With devotion, determination, and the grace of the guru, we can ascend these five steps to find the ultimate fulfillment we are all seeking.

With joy,
NAYASWAMI DEVI

72
May 17, 2018

WE DON'T
KNOW ENOUGH

One of the Ananda teachers just sent me an article about the physiological link between the breath and a brain chemical, noradrenaline. Here's a quote from the article:

> The research shows for the first time that breathing — a key element of meditation and mindfulness practices — directly affects the levels of a natural chemical messenger in the brain called noradrenaline. This chemical messenger is released when we are challenged, curious, exercised, focused or emotionally aroused, and, if produced at the right levels, helps the brain grow new connections, like a brain fertilizer. The way we breathe, in other words, directly affects the chemistry of our brains in a way that can enhance our attention and improve our brain health.

The study goes on to say that passively observing the breath (a mindfulness technique) helps to increase attention, while controlling the breath (pranayama) helps us either activate or calm the mind as needed. On the Ananda path we do both of these: In the Hong-Sau technique we simply observe the breath, whereas with Kriya we actively control the breath. These two together not only lead to deeper meditation, but also help to balance and improve brain functioning.

I find these kinds of studies to be very interesting and helpful tools for explaining meditation. But they also need to be tak-

en cautiously, because they are limited to the physical plane and can lead to the mistaken perception that it is the brain that produces awareness. With the current materialistic bias in science, it's important to recognize that physiological processes don't *cause* the changes in consciousness, but rather *reflect* them. Otherwise it would be like saying, "The heart rate and legs speed up, which causes the mind to decide to run."

Yoga, including asanas, the Energization Exercises, and meditation, works with subtle energies, not merely physical ones. Yogis have long taught that the breath, mind, and prana are interrelated, and that our consciousness extends far beyond the brain and the physical realm. Great masters of many paths, after all, demonstrate the ability to consciously exit and reenter the body.

In *Autobiography of a Yogi*, Paramhansa Yogananda says:

> The mystery of life and death, whose solution is the only purpose of man's sojourn on earth, is intimately interwoven with breath. Breathlessness is deathlessness. Realizing this truth, the ancient rishis of India seized on the sole clue of the breath and developed a precise and rational science of breathlessness. Had India no other gift for the world, *Kriya Yoga* alone would suffice as a kingly offering.

Great yogis who can control both breath and consciousness can also manipulate the physical plane: they can levitate, manifest objects, and perceive thoughts at a distance. Lacking their consciousness, we think of these things as miracles.

As beginners, there is a great deal that we simply don't understand, and that is why we need a teacher to increase our awareness of these subtle realms. The best course is to attune ourselves to the guru and ask him to reveal these deeper truths to us. To his sincere disciples, Yogananda emphasized attunement above all else. He could guide those who were open to him, and he will guide us still even though he is no longer present on the physical plane.

So, fascinating though these brain studies are, let's understand that they are but a small part of a much more intricate and beautiful story of spiritual evolution.

In joy,
NAYASWAMI JYOTISH

P.S. You can read the article at <u>joyiswith.in/6</u>.

73
May 24, 2018

The PHILOSOPHER KING

We were once talking with Swami Kriyananda about the best form of government. "Enlightened monarchy with a philosopher king is the highest expression," he said. "But it's only possible in a more advanced age in which mass consciousness is higher than it is today."

For me Swamiji was a true philosopher king. As we celebrated the anniversary of his birthday on May 19, many devotees shared stories of how he had uplifted their life.

I remember sitting around a campfire one evening in a forest glade at the Meditation Retreat, listening to him play his guitar and sing some of his beautiful songs. As I gazed up at the stars, I was transported to a realm of nobility and divine consciousness that I knew was my real soul home.

For me that evening, and for everyone he met, Swamiji was ennobling, wise, compassionate — a man of dignity, vision, and inspiration. Even though we were the merest of spiritual beginners when the first generation of Ananda members came in the late 1960s, he made each of us feel our deep inner worth.

Swamiji gave me my spiritual name, "Devi," in an unexpected way that also challenged me to live up to my highest potential. I was having lunch with a friend at a restaurant in Nevada City, California, when Swamiji walked in and came over. "I'm going to give you the name 'Devi,'" he said. "It means 'Divine Mother,' and you'd better live up to it." Through all the many years since then, I have felt him inwardly guiding me in how best to "live up to it."

Everyone he met was welcomed into his kingdom of joy.

His dignity and nobility were always balanced with humility. Once we were walking with Swamiji in a shopping mall in Sacramento, California, and he began telling us about a letter he'd received. Its author had praised Swamiji as a leader, a spiritual teacher, and a writer. Kriyananda said to us, "I could see that he felt he would never be able to accomplish such things himself. He needs to understand that I've just been doing this longer than the rest of you. All of you can do what I've done."

Throughout his life this "philosopher king" expressed tremendous generosity of spirit. Anyone who came to him for spiritual training—everyone he met, in fact—was welcomed into his kingdom of joy. The countless dinners, social gatherings, P. G. Wodehouse readings, and informal teas that he hosted for devotees around the world were his way of making everyone feel included in his divine friendship.

But this generous, welcoming, noble consciousness didn't end when Swamiji left his body in 2013. Play, or even better, sing his music. Read his books. Listen to his talks. Meditate on his words. Even now he is inviting each sincere devotee to enter his kingdom.

And what is his kingdom? It is the joy-filled realm of God-consciousness, which he attained through discipleship to his guru, Paramhansa Yogananda. It is timeless and eternal, yet reachable at any moment by anyone whose heart and mind are open to God's all-transforming love.

With gratitude for his gifts to us all,
NAYASWAMI DEVI

74
May 31, 2018

GAME OVER

The traditional yin-yang symbol.

The major premise of Paramhansa Yogananda's first book, *The Science of Religion*, is that everyone in the world shares the same basic motivation: to be happy and to avoid pain. I've been reading a book with a similar theme, *12 Rules for Life: An Antidote to Chaos*, by a psychologist and philosopher, Jordan B. Peterson. His theme is similar to Yogananda's, but he states it slightly differently: Life is a quest to maintain order and avoid chaos.

He has an interesting explanation of the well-known yin-yang symbol. The white half, he says, represents order, and the black half, chaos. We (and all living things) constantly tread the winding line between the two forces, striving to create and maintain order while challenged by an unstable world that causes chaos. Order allows us to live and prosper, while chaos brings the threat of ruin and death. The small dot of the opposite color in each side represents the potential for transformation.

Most approaches, including Peterson's 12 rules, are intended to show us how better to navigate our challenges—to be healthier, wealthier, and happier. But as we progress to higher spiritual levels, we begin to tire of this limited reality. We yearn, then, for a guide who can show us the way out, one who has experienced his own consciousness beyond the limitations of the dream. He can teach us how to find the exit and the bliss-filled realms that exist beyond the world of maya.

Yogis must balance these two goals: Our teachings will, indeed, help us live successfully in this world of maya, but, more importantly, they also show us how to achieve unity (moksha) and escape altogether from the dream of duality. Our job, spiritually speaking, is to overcome the chaos caused by ego consciousness.

Master often spoke of this world as being like a dream or movie. Today, he might have used the analogy of a video game. Imagine a complex and incredibly addictive game, called "Life." If we were thrust into a game with no memory of previous ones, we could be fooled into thinking that the current "incarnation" was all that existed. As long as we stay within the game of duality, we must play by its rules, which are designed to keep the game entertaining by threatening our order with chaos. As long as we are entertained, we will keep hitting the button that says, "Play Again?"

The exit can be found only by detaching ourselves from our identity in the game. This we do by stilling the breath, and withdrawing the mind and heart from outer stimulation, and from their addictions. Finally, in deep meditation, we see and pass through the exit door—the spiritual eye. Then the illusion vanishes, and our soul awakes to the realization that it has been stuck in a dream, a self-enclosed circle of yin and yang. When that deep awakening comes, we are ready to return at last to our true home. Only then will we opt for the button that says, "Game Over."

In joy,
NAYASWAMI JYOTISH

75

June 7, 2018

HOW to WATER a GARDEN

My alarm clock went off in the early hours each morning. Though it was still dark and often cold, I knew that if I didn't get up immediately, I'd be late. My small trailer had no electricity or running water; I'd light a kerosene lamp, wash up with water from a gallon jug I carried home each day, and then sit to meditate.

"These remain among the greatest joys of my life."

My meditation completed, after grabbing a quick breakfast I'd rush off to meet our head gardener, Haanel Cassidy, at 7:00 a.m. to catch a ride to start the workday on the farm. Haanel had had a lifetime of experience in organic gardening, with some seventy years to his credit, and had become a dear friend and mentor. He would always be there waiting in his green Toyota pickup truck, "Tigger."

So began each day during my first years at Ananda Village. Working with people who were to become my lifelong friends, and learning gardening skills from Haanel—these remain among the greatest joys of my life.

We didn't need to look far to see spiritual lessons in almost everything we learned about raising vegetables. The climate at Ananda village is one of extremes: it's either constant rain or drought. Watering the cultivated acres during the long dry season was always a challenge. Here are some things I learned about life from watering our gardens.

Connect to a Source. All of our irrigation was done with gravity-fed water lines from reservoirs higher up than the gardens. Keeping the water system functioning and in good repair required our constant attention.

Lesson: If you want to grow spiritually, look for people of higher wisdom, keep a good inward connection with them, and have the humility to allow them constantly to water your consciousness.

Channel the water where you want it to go. The vegetable beds were set on a slight downward slope, so that gravity would draw the water from the top to the bottom. With our hoes, we'd dig one main trench across the top of the bed, and then smaller trenches feeding off of it leading to each row. Each day we'd open or close the smaller trenches to allow the water to flow where it was needed.

Lesson: Life is full of choices: Direct your energy to where you will spiritually benefit the most, and block off the other options.

Watch out for impediments to the flow. Sometimes if we were inattentive, we didn't notice that a rock or lump of soil had fallen into a trench and was diverting the water. Later we'd come back to discover the vegetable rows were still dry, while the weeds around the garden were sitting in big, muddy pools.

Lesson: Always be on the watch for harmful attitudes or habits that are blocking the flow of your energy. That energy must go somewhere, and usually finds its way along the course of least resistance.

Be sure to water the whole garden. We had to pay close attention to ensure that every row was getting the moisture it needed, so that the entire garden could flourish. Gardens are most productive and happiest when every plant is getting what is required.

Lesson: Live a balanced life. Don't neglect any area, but sure make that all aspects — body, mind, and soul — are getting the energy they need.

In these ways I learned that God can be found in watering gardens, for His presence is everywhere. As our guru, Paramhansa Yogananda, wrote: "Like a silent, invisible river flowing beneath the desert, flows the vast dimensionless river of Spirit through the sands of time, through the sands of experience, and through the sands of all souls."

May the flow of divine grace always water your soul.
NAYASWAMI DEVI

76
June 14, 2018

ANIMALS *and* COMPASSION

When I was young, one of the most important members of our family was Nipper. He was a medium-sized dog with amazingly intelligent eyes, a golden coat, and a combination of the best traits of numerous breeds. He was a faithful playmate, protector, and coconspirator during my daily adventures. Many people remember a beloved four-legged friend who shared their youth, although none (I am sad to have to break this to you) can have been quite so glorious as Nipper.

Our house was across the street from a large park that served as a picnic spot in our small Midwestern town. In the center of the park was a large playground, and among Nipper's many talents was a mastery of the sliding chute. On Sundays, when the park was filled, Nipper would prance over to the playground to begin his show—ceaselessly climbing the high ladder and sliding down the chute. Naturally, a crowd would soon form, cheering him on, although such an exhibitionist as he needed little encouragement. My brother and I would stand in the back of the crowd too embarrassed to admit that this was our dog, but too proud of Nipper to leave. You know the feeling.

Pets are our teachers, acting as mirrors for our behavior. All faiths have a variation of the Golden Rule: "Do unto others as you would have them do unto you." A sincere practice

of this simple statement should include not only people, but all life. In the Gospel of St. Matthew we find this famous passage:

> "For I was hungry, and you gave me food; I was thirsty, and you gave me drink; I was a stranger, and you welcomed me; I was naked, and you clothed me; I was sick, and you visited me; I was in prison, and you came to me." Then the righteous will answer him, saying, "Lord, when did we see you hungry and feed you, or thirsty and give you drink? And when did we see you a stranger and welcome you, or naked and clothe you? And when did we see you sick, or in prison, and visit you?" And the King will answer them, "Truly, I say to you, as you did it to one of the least of these my brothers, you did it to me."

Our love for God should be given equally whether He is masquerading as a beggar, a dog, a cat, an ocean, or a rainforest. Perhaps God gives us pets as first lessons in love and compassion, before we move on to the more complex task of loving other people, or even ourselves.

We recently attended a fundraising dinner put on by the Guibord Center, an interfaith work in Los Angeles dedicated to building bridges and fostering respect among various spiritual expressions. The highlight of the evening was a short film about how various traditions treat animals. (I've included below a link to the trailer; the film itself is available there as well.)

Life should be a glorious experience of giving and receiving love, which animals do so naturally. We would have longer and happier lives were we to heed the advice of a bumper sticker I once saw: "I wish I were the kind of person my dog thinks I am."

In joy,
NAYASWAMI JYOTISH

P.S. You can view the Guibord Center trailer and film at this link: joyiswith.in/8.

A DAY of YOGA

Over ten thousand people gathered on the grounds of the iconic India Gate in Delhi, India; at the same time many thousands congregated at the United Nations Plaza in New York City. Why had they all come? Was it part of some global political protest? Yes and No.

It was June 21, the annual International Day of Yoga created by the United Nations in December 2014. In Delhi, New York, and many other places around the world people had assembled simply to practice yoga asanas together, and to affirm this year's theme: "Yoga for Peace."

It's important for people seeking higher consciousness and peace on earth to join together, showing the unity of all people on this quest. And we can make every day of our life a "day of yoga," if we understand it in a deeper way.

For "yoga" means "union": uniting the individual soul with God through techniques, right attitudes, deep meditation, and devotion. Thus yoga is much more than just asanas, and should incorporate every aspect of our existence.

From Vedic times in India, the great sages taught an ideal scheme of life that embraced four stages from youth to old age

"Devotion," by Nayaswami Jyotish.

leading us to true "yoga." Let's call these four stages the student, the householder, the advisor, and the free wanderer.* Each one can also be thought of as a part of the day to keep focused on God in that particular way.

The Student Stage

As you awaken each morning, train yourself to have your first thoughts be filled with devotion—to God, to a saint, or to whatever inspires you. If you can keep your mind spiritually focused and open to higher guidance before you become engaged in other activities, your whole day will be uplifted. Here are some words from Paramhansa Yogananda's beautiful "Prayer at Dawn": "With the opening of the earliest dawn and the lotus-buds, my soul softly opens in prayer to receive Thy light. Bathe each petal of my mind with Thy radiant rays!"

The Householder Stage

After morning meditation, we move into the busy activities of the day to fulfill our responsibilities. Even though we are outwardly engaged, we can see and remember God in everything we do, and perform our duties with calmness and joy in service to Him. In Yoganandaji's "Prayer at Noon," he writes: "As the sun shines in the busiest streets, so may I behold Thy rays of protecting love in the crowded places of my life's activities."

The Advisor Stage

In this phase of life we begin to withdraw from involvement in outer activities. Our duty now is to serve in an advisory and training role for others. So as this "day of yoga" draws towards dusk, we can mentally detach ourselves from activity, and relax once more into the peace of meditation. In "Prayer at Eventide," Yoganandaji says: "The day is done. Refreshed and sanctified with the sunshine of the day I pass through the portals of evening, dimly

---

* If you want to know more about these stages, we recommend a new book from Crystal Clarity Publishers: *The Four Stages of Yoga*, by Nischala Cryer.

adorned with faint stars, to enter into the temple of silence and worship Thee."

The Free Wanderer

The final stage is for the seeker to free himself from all worldly concerns and focus completely on the search for God. Our "day of yoga" has been completed. As we close our eyes in sleep, we can offer all of our activities and thoughts, successes and failures up to God. Thus we release our sense of egoic separation into longing for oneness with the Divine. In our Guru's "Prayer at Night," we find these words: "One by one I have closed the doors of my senses lest the fragrance of the rose or the song of the nightingale distract my love from Thee. I have left everything—but, where art Thou? Come, show Thyself!"

In these ways, every day can bring us closer to divine union. And a lifetime filled with such days is one that fulfills our true spiritual destiny.

Towards unity with God,
NAYASWAMI DEVI

78
June 28, 2018

ACTING on INTUITION

Intuitive insights come to each of us. They are, after all, the soul's way of perceiving. Sometimes they come as a clear knowing; at other times, as a hunch; and often as just a whisper of feeling. True intuition is God's way of guiding us, but most of us ignore our intuitions most of the time. This last weekend we saw a remarkable validation of what happens when, in spite of all obstacles, you act on your intuition.

Janakidevi has always been a woman with strong intuition. She lives at Laurelwood, an Ananda community near Portland, Oregon. Age was beginning to take its toll, and she was starting to lose her sense of purpose and hope. Then one morning in meditation she received the strong message that she should build a sanctuary in nature where people could come to pray, but ignored the thought as just another of what she calls her "zany" ideas. A few days later, however, the impulse came back even more strongly, and she clearly saw a larger than life-sized statue of Yogananda surrounded by beautiful gardens.

Rainbow bowing down to the statue of Yogananda.

She began taking a step at a time to realize her vision. And—this is very important if you want to accomplish anything big—she didn't stop taking those steps even though at the age of eighty-five she felt that the project was beyond her abilities. Her enthusiasm soon attracted helpers: her husband, Byasa; a wonderful sculptor, Gary Roller, who was having similar intuitions; and many others who were also willing to donate money and time.

Source: KentWilliamsPhotography.com.

Last Saturday, at Ananda Laurelwood, we unveiled the eight-foot statue. There was an amazing sense of grace, as if the bronze was permeated with Master's presence. Everyone felt that this would be a place of pilgrimage for countless years ahead, and two days later a rainbow blessing added to the feeling. There are lessons here for all of us.

Be open to your intuitions: Yogananda said, "Tune yourself with the creative power of spirit. You will be in contact with the Infinite Intelligence that is able to guide you and solve all problems. Power from the dynamic source of your being will flow uninterruptedly so that you will be able to perform creatively in any sphere of activity."

Strengthen your intuition: Intuition usually speaks to us in whispers rather than shouts, and you must quiet your desires and thoughts to hear them more clearly. These subtle messages sometimes come with subconscious longings mixed in, so be wary of any ideas that aren't accompanied by a feeling of calmness and humility. Intuition's feeling should be more "Thank you" than "Oh, boy!"

Act on your intuition: The more you act, the stronger its power becomes. Take a step at a time, and keep checking in to feel if you are on the right track. When your intuition is truly from the Divine Intelligence, it will continue to guide you. If your power of intuition is well developed then you can act more confidently: At his school in Ranchi, India, Yogananda had a vision calling him to America — and left that very afternoon!

Great things can happen: It would not be a stretch to say that all great works are built on the foundation of intuition. Be open. Be trusting. Be persistent. You never know what the Divine wants to accomplish through you.

In joy,
NAYASWAMI JYOTISH

79

July 5, 2018

EVERYTHING BALANCES OUT *in the* END

"But, that's so unfair!" How many times have you spoken these words, or at least had this thought? I know I often have. Maybe someone else got the praise for something that you did. Or maybe you got the blame for something you didn't do. It's hard to resist this thought when we see ruthless, selfish people gaining power over others, while honest, selfless people are left to struggle. Then it's all too easy to lose faith and become cynical.

It was probably just such a reaction that led someone to comment, "No good deed goes unpunished." When a devotee shared this statement with Swami Kriyananda, he corrected him, saying, "No, that's not so. It would be truer to say, 'No good deed goes *unnoticed.*'"

Recently I heard a wonderful story in this regard from the annals of India. There are many tales about Lord Krishna traveling with his devotee, Narada, giving him spiritual instruction along the way. In this account, Krishna and Narada are wandering through the countryside disguised as beggars, and they happen upon a town. Dusty and hungry, they come to the splendid house of a prosperous merchant, whom they ask for food. With heartless indifference, he coldly drives them away, saying, "Get you

hence, you worthless beggars. I have nothing for you." Narada looks at Krishna, but Krishna only smiles.

Eventually, on the outskirts of the town they come to the poor mud hut of an old farmer. He lives alone and has little to offer them, but kindly invites them to take rest in his hut. His one possession is an old cow, which he proceeds to milk; he then offers all the milk to the two beggars. Narada looks again at Krishna, who says nothing, but stares reflectively off into the distance.

The next day as they are leaving, they stop for water at the local well, and are surprised to find the townspeople all aflutter with some news. "Have you heard?" they ask. "The rich merchant had a big financial windfall and has doubled his wealth, while the poor farmer's cow died, leaving him with nothing."

This turn of fortune is too much for Narada. He pulls Krishna aside and cries, "My Lord, how can you allow such injustice? The rich man had plenty to spare, but he gave us nothing, and now he gets more riches. Yet the poor farmer gave us everything he had, and now he loses even his one possession. This seems so unfair!"

Krishna smiles again, and this time he speaks. "The rich man believes that wealth and possessions will bring him happiness, so by receiving yet more, he will learn the more quickly that only suffering comes from worldly attachments. The poor farmer has great devotion for God, but his old cow was his last attachment. Now his soul is free." Looking tenderly into Narada's eyes, Krishna concludes, "Remember, the ways of God are filled with love and wisdom, and everything balances in the end."

Patience, inner strength, devotion, and trust in God: these are attitudes that help us find peace and understanding in this confusing world of mirages. So the next time you're tempted to think something is unfair, replace that thought with this one: "God is in charge of this world, and is lovingly bringing to each soul just what they need to find their freedom."

With joy,
NAYASWAMI DEVI

80
July 12, 2018

The MOST IMPORTANT THING I DO

In 1979 Ananda began a period of expansion, and Devi and I helped start a large ashram in San Francisco. An early challenge was to find ways to support ourselves, especially in a way that allowed us to serve together. One solution we found was a business with a vegetarian restaurant on the first floor and a small bookstore on the second. Vairagi was the manager, and after closing up each night she had to take a bus across town through some of the poorest parts of the city. She hated it. The late-night ride was frightening and upsetting for a single woman, especially when there were intoxicated passengers. She came to Swami Kriyananda and shared her plight.

He asked, "Is there any other way for you to get home? Can you drive or get a ride?"

"No, I can't drive, and there is no one I can rely on to take me."

"Can you take a cab?" Swamiji continued.

"No, it's too expensive," she replied.

Then Swamiji gave her this advice. "If the bus is the only way, then when you get on, pick out the most troubled person and pray for him or her during the whole trip. If that person gets off before you are home, choose another."

A couple of weeks later Vairagi came to Swamiji again, not with complaints this time, but to tell him that the bus ride was now her favorite part of the day. Sometimes a little piece of advice can flip a situation, or a life.

We recently had a satsang with the younger residents at Ananda Village during which we asked the group this question: "What is one thing you do regularly that you find really helpful spiritually?" Here were some of the answers:

> "During the day, especially when I'm having a challenge, I try to remember how I felt during my morning meditation."

> "I stand up straight and constantly repeat, 'Jai Guru.'"

> "When I am out and about I try to pray for everyone I see. It quickly brings me back to my center." Another said something similar: "I try to give love to everyone I see."

> "Because I struggle with low self-esteem, when I get down on myself I try to think of several things I do well or that I like about myself."

> A musician said, "In my mind I am constantly singing a chant or one of Swami Kriyananda's songs."

> "Before I will leave a meditation, I always make sure to form a personal heart-connection with the guru."

These are only a few of the many ideas that were offered that evening. Each of us has some unique habit or attitude that helps us spiritually, and it can be extremely helpful to share these with one another. Ask yourself, "What is the most important thing I do?" and share the answer with a receptive friend. It may be exactly what they need, and go on to become the favorite part of their day.

In divine friendship,
NAYASWAMI JYOTISH

"*Green River Valley Sunrise,*"
photo by Swami Kriyananda.

81
July 19, 2018

LEAVING *the* MORGUE

As I entered the chemistry lab on the basement floor of the hospital, no one was there to greet me, only racks of dirty test tubes. My part-time job during my last semester in college was to clean the vials after the chemists had left for the day.

It wasn't very interesting work. I usually found myself alone in a lifeless room lit by flickering fluorescent lights.

And unfortunately, the lab environment was pretty toxic: All the racks of test tubes had to be lowered into a large acid vat before they were washed. The fumes from the acid were mostly drawn off by a ventilating hood, but I didn't feel I was adding years to my life by working around it.

To make matters worse, when I went into the hallway to find a restroom, I saw a hospital orderly pushing a large cart. In the dim light, at first I couldn't tell what was on it, but then as he drew nearer, I realized that the cart held a corpse covered with a sheet. Taken aback, I stepped aside to watch him enter the morgue right across the hall from the lab.

The whole experience was about as devoid of life as you could get, but there was one consolation. At this time a wonderful audio cassette had been released: *West Meets East*, improvisation sessions between the great Indian sitarist, Ravi Shankar, and the violin virtuoso, Yehudi Menuhin. I'd bring a cassette player with me to the lab, play that tape for hours, and revel in the rich, soulful music.

The contrast between the sterile, lifeless lab and the transcendent, joy-filled music awakened within me a great longing to feel such inspiration all the time. I began to realize that life, even at its best, was like a morgue compared to the inner world of the soul.

A month later a friend handed me a copy of *Autobiography of a Yogi* by Paramhansa Yogananda and told me about Ananda, which was based on his teachings. Thus, almost fifty years ago, I began my spiritual journey.

For each of us the way is different, yet it's basically the same. Here are some stages of the journey that may help guide you.

To begin a journey, you must want to move forward from where you presently are. As long as you're content with your circumstances, you'll never be motivated to get started. What motivates us? It differs from person to person: perhaps it's unhappiness; or longing for truth; or seeking to know who we really are. In any case, the longing for something more is the impetus that spurs us onward. Remember what has motivated you, and keep seeking it until you reach your goal.

To move away from the familiar, you need a map or guide. It's very difficult to find our way forward without someone who knows the terrain. For this we need a guru and his teachings to guide us. Maybe you'll ask: But what if I don't have a guru? When the seeker is ready, the guru will come. So it's important to know our own limitations in directing our steps, and sincerely to ask for personal, divine guidance to show us the way. Once you've found your guide, continue to follow his directions.

As you continue your journey, try to lighten your load. You can't move forward with lots of unneeded baggage, such as old habits, ways of thinking, and self-definitions. Leave behind anything you don't need, and simplify your life to what you really want to bring with you into the future.

Remember, this journey is one of self-discovery. You're not actually moving through time and space, but traveling within to reconnect with your true Self. As far as the journey may seem to take you, you'll always return to the point from which you started—

To begin a journey, you must want to move forward from where you presently are.

your inner home in God. So this journey isn't really about traveling at all, but simply remembering what we've always known: who and what we really are.

Once we make this discovery, our real life begins: one of such inner richness, beauty, freedom, and joy that nothing, not even death, can ever destroy it. We thrill, then, to the music of our soul, which was playing all the time.

With joy,
NAYASWAMI DEVI

82
July 26, 2018

WHAT SHOULD I DO?

What should I do? This is the question we hear most frequently. It might take the form of "What should I do about a short temper?" or "What should I do about my mind wandering during meditation?" Simply asking "What should I do?" means that you're ready to move beyond passivity and engage your willpower. Congratulate yourself whenever you ask this question, because you are halfway to the solution.

Here is some general advice:

1. Start with externals: It is easier to control physical things than thoughts, so start there. Feel sluggish? Then stand up straight and breathe deeply for one minute, or do one or two energization exercises. Feeling sad? Put on some uplifting music, read something inspirational, or find a way to help someone else. Do you have trouble meditating regularly? Go to a satsang or take a class in person or online. Is your mind restless during your meditations? Start by keeping your body absolutely still. You get the point: For every problem there will be an external practice that will get you started in the right direction.

2. Think positively: It is a little harder to control your thoughts, but it is doable. Positive thinking creates a flow of prana and has a domino effect that includes beneficial results for the brain and hormones. The key is to derail negative thought patterns before they have a

Paramhansa Yogananda giving a devotee a blessing.

chance to gather momentum. Many people find that a simple affirmation will neutralize the problem, especially if they repeat it as soon as the first thought arises. It also helps to bring your mind to the spiritual eye with a surge of upward energy. Perhaps the single most helpful practice is to develop the habit of being grateful. Thank God for everything, including when a challenge arises.

3. Enlist the help of God and Gurus. Paramhansa Yogananda said that our part is only 25% of what is needed. The guru does another 25% of the work on our behalf and God does the other 50%. That means that calling on them for help is four times as effective as trying to do it on your own. Try to connect deeply with God in meditation, and then keep that contact alive throughout the day.

In my last blog I asked people to describe the practices they find most spiritually helpful, and we received nearly eighty replies. Nothing can be a substitute for reading the responses themselves and seeing the richness of practical and inspiring advice, but here are five themes mentioned most often:

1. I practice gratitude.
2. I pray to God in meditation and ask His advice during the day.
3. I repeat an affirmation or mantra.
4. I attune to Master through visualizing him or gazing at his photo with deep attention.
5. I feel that God is acting through me in every activity.

I suggest that you read the responses* and make a list of those things you find most personally helpful. Then, when you are wondering, "What should I do?" you will have a place to start.

In joy,
NAYASWAMI JYOTISH

---

* The responses are listed at <u>joyiswith.in/9</u>.

WE ARE BUILDING
a TEMPLE of LIGHT

The sun rose an unnatural shade of red-orange in the hazy early morning sky. Though the burning forests and towns were hundreds of miles from Ananda Village, the wind was blowing the smoke in our direction. The air quality was unhealthy and the temperatures were high, but still they came. *They were building a temple of light.*

Devotees from all the Ananda communities in America had come for a special Seva Week to help erect the new temple. Some were skilled carpenters; others were merely willing and happy to do whatever they could. Some were young; others were older. Some were people we'd known for years; others were new to Ananda. Some came alone, while others came in groups. There were even four father-son teams. Many wore face masks to filter out the smoke in the air, but the heat and the haze didn't matter: *They are building a temple of light.*

As we talked with them during the morning break, I deeply felt how important this temple is — not just for those who are part of Ananda, but for

Source: *Kent Williams Photography.com.*

the whole planet. Maybe we can't put out forest fires, or reverse climate change, or bring dharma into government and politics, but this much we can do: *We can build a temple of light.*

Our guru, Paramhansa Yogananda, said, "Don't try to banish darkness by beating at it with a stick. Turn on the light, and the darkness will vanish as though it had never been." In other words, the darkness in the world today can't be destroyed by a head-on attack. Our most effective weapon in this fight is consciously to draw divine light into our lives. This light itself is the only power that can dispel darkness.

Every God-attuned thought, word, feeling, and action we have illumines a small part of the world, and diminishes the darkness. Every seen or unseen act of kindness, compassion, or selflessness helps to empower this light. When collectively we lift our own consciousness and help others to do the same, we also strengthen that power. *Then we, too, are building a temple of light.*

Build this temple in your workplace, your home, your family, your meditation room, and most importantly in your own heart. Though there be challenges before you, forge ahead with determination until the foundation of your temple is solid. With your inner strength, erect the supporting beams and walls to give it shape. With your undying aspirations, raise the soaring roof. With garlands of loving devotion, decorate the altar. Finally, invite everyone to enter and receive the radiant light of your inner temple.

The word "guru" derives from root words meaning "dispeller of darkness." *Together, then, with God and Guru, let us build a temple of light that spans the globe.*

Your friend in God,
NAYASWAMI DEVI

84
Aug. 9, 2018

TOOLS *for* LIVING

Let me set the scene: an amphitheater packed with several hundred people while, in the background, the bare wood of an emerging temple rises miraculously. People from many nations immersing themselves in the teachings of Paramhansa Yogananda and Swami Kriyananda. Add stirring music, drama, friendship, joy, and light. Here, for a brief transformative week, the astral plane has touched the earth. It is Spiritual Renewal Week at Ananda Village.

The theme for the week is *The Power of Self-Transformation*, and Devi and I talked about the tools that can help us. One of the listeners told us, "I was furiously scribbling notes but I'm afraid that I might have missed important points. Can you review them in a written form?" So, here is a brief summary of my part of the class. (Devi will share hers next week.)

God manifests creation by vibrating a small part of his awareness. Vibration creates duality: the positive and negative charges in the atom, the light and dark of images in a movie. For us, as humans, this primordial duality manifests as the breath, as pleasure and pain, as good and evil. On a subtler level, duality manifests as movement of energy, either upward or downward, in our astral spine. As energy moves down, the ego, the material world, temptations, and self-serving attitudes are strengthened. As the energy moves in an upward direction, the world of spirit grows more real. It would be fair to say that all spiritual techniques and attitudes are meant to strengthen and maintain an upward flow of life-force toward the spiritual eye where enlightenment awaits.

Paramhansa Yogananda explained that all of the characters in the Bhagavad Gita are personifications of inner tendencies. The great war that takes place is the battle between the positive and negative citizens of our mental kingdom. When our life-force is flowing downward, we energize "King Material Desire" and his ninety-nine brothers, representing the contractive egoic tendencies. A positive upward flow supports our spiritual qualities, characterized by the five Pandava brothers, who symbolize the chakras.

I will reason, I will will, I will act, but guide Thou my reason, will, and activity to the right path in everything.

For the seeker, the question is how to strengthen that upward flow. The tools available to us are reason, willpower, and action. Rightly directed they send the energy upward toward enlightenment; wrongly directed they lead to sense slavery. Yogananda said that the highest prayer is to call on God's help in this way: "I will reason, I will will, I will act, but guide Thou my reason, will, and activity to the right path in everything."

When reason is positive and inspired, will strong and focused, and activity properly channeled, energy rises in the spine. As it does, each chakra is empowered, and we experience the stages of Patanjali's eightfold path. Successively these are *yama*, the power to resist temptation; *niyama*, the power to adhere to virtue; *asana*, fiery self-control; *pranayama*, the ability to turn the heart's energy upward toward God; and *pratyahara*, calmness and expansion that come from sense detachment. Ultimately, all of the upward-flowing energy must be offered into the light of the guru at the spiritual eye.

When reason, will, and activity are negatively directed, the opposite occurs. Our spiritual aspirations wane and we become increasingly negative and self-centered. We experience agitation, moodiness, and an inability to control our own behavior, with a consequent inclination towards trying to control the behavior of others. We shun virtue while being drawn toward tawdry temptation.

This is a quick summary of the battle for Self-realization. Yogananda reminded us that "The minutes are more important than the years." Every day offers hundreds of opportunities to make small choices that send our life-force in either an upward or downward direction.

Fortunately, God is on our side in this battle. Invoke His help with this affirmation from Master: "I go forth in perfect faith in the power of Omnipresent Good to bring me what I need at the time I need it."

In joy,
NAYASWAMI JYOTISH

P.S. The full class can be viewed at joyiswith.in/11. And the collection of all the week's talks, at joyiswith.in/10.

85
Aug. 16, 2018

HOW to BUILD INNER POWER

"There is a hidden strength within me to overcome all obstacles. I will bring forth that indomitable power and energy." Paramhansa Yogananda shared this formidable thought with us, and gave us tools to accomplish that great goal. Here are five effective ways to build our inner power.

1. Begin with Self-Analysis

Introspection is a tool of which Yoganandaji spoke repeatedly. Analyze with self-honesty your own strengths and weaknesses. Once you've identified them, give increased energy to developing your strong points—these are your best warriors in the battle against downward-pulling forces. Practice daily by bringing your strengths to the fore.

Then, without self-denial or justification, look at your weaknesses. At the first sign of their whining in the back of your mind, cut these weaklings off at the source, and refuse to allow them to dictate to you. As Sri Yukteswar said, "Roam in the world as a lion of self-control. Don't let the frogs of weakness kick you around!" Whenever you find yourself justifying your mistakes or blaming them on others, know that you are diminishing your own inner power, and stop immediately.

2. Practice Even-mindedness and Detachment

Controlling the reactive process is one of the central teachings of yoga. Circumstances are always neutral. If, for example, we al-

I'm seated beside Swami Kriyananda at his birthday celebration around 2005.

low ourselves to react when it's too hot or too cold outside, we are constantly a victim of circumstances over which we have no control. Remember: Nothing and no one can take away your peace if you don't allow it. When you find yourself being pulled into a reactive vortex, repeat these words of Yoganandaji: "I am the prince of perpetual peace, playing in a drama of sad and happy dreams on the stage of experience."

3. Develop Mental Strength

Concentration and determination are the foundations upon which we build the edifice of inner power. Challenge yourself daily to accomplish something new, or to perform a routine task in a different way. When working towards a goal, don't allow into your mind the thought, "Well, it's good enough." Continue on until you can say honestly, "I've done the best that I can."

When we live in this way, we draw the support of the universe to infuse our own efforts. Try to feel that with the magnetism of your determination, there are no obstacles that you can't overcome.

4. Love Heroically

Swami Kriyananda has said that when times are difficult, either for you personally or in the world around you, the best way to stand strong is to love heroically. In a sense, this is the combination of detachment and mental strength. If you can love others no matter how they act towards you, then you can transform personal love and friendship to expressions of God's divine love. Try it. Don't hold back your love from anyone, friend or foe, and feel the power and freedom that this awakens within you.

5. Find Your Own Relationship with God's Light

The times in which we live are confusing, to say the least. So many claims vie boastfully one against another that universal

"The world may change or disappear, but truth can never die!"

values and truth have become obscured. But as Swami Kriyananda declares in one of his songs: "The world may change or disappear, but truth can never die!"

In these uncertain times, we need especially to follow the practices of meditation that we've been given. The truth, the light, and the love we are seeking are all to be found within the calmness of our own being. Once you've touched these inner realities, cling to them and don't waver. They will be the divine beacon that guides you through all adversity. As we build our own inner power, we can also become a source of support and strength to all those around us.

In divine friendship,
NAYASWAMI DEVI

LIVING a LIFE of DISCIPLESHIP

"The characteristic features of Indian culture have long been a search for ultimate verities and the concomitant disciple-guru relationship." Thus begins Paramhansa Yogananda's world-famous *Autobiography of a Yogi*.

Millions have read these immortal words, but few have lived them. One who did was Swami Kriyananda. By the force of his example he founded a movement and inspired millions. Now, a movie, *The Answer*—a living portrayal of the disciple-guru relationship—is about to be released. The first part of the film depicts Swamiji's desperate search for truth. Then, in scene after moving scene, his yearning is finally satisfied, all the answers he'd ever sought coming through the love and wisdom of his great master, Paramhansa Yogananda. This film is the best visual expression of discipleship I have ever seen. I am not alone in my reaction. Very few people have been able to sit through the movie without tears of joy glistening in their eyes.

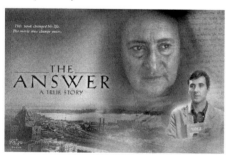

There seems to be a special grace behind the release of *The Answer*. Perhaps it's a reflection of the times in which we find ourselves, and because the film is one way for God to fulfill the promise He made in the Bhagavad Gita:

"Whenever virtue declines and vice predominates, I incarnate on earth. Taking visible form, I come to destroy evil and reestablish virtue." Whatever the cause, there is a special energy surrounding the release of this film.

One way that grace has manifested is through Sri Rajinikanth, the Indian movie superstar, who has given a moving testimonial for the film. He is a disciple of Paramhansa Yogananda and Babaji, and was deeply affected when he viewed it recently. For those who are not familiar with him, Rajinikanth is widely considered the most popular and revered actor in India. (We have included a link to his testimonial at the end of the blog.) A second highly acclaimed India actor, Victor Banerjee, plays the role of Yoganandaji in the film.

Another demonstration of grace is the array of prestigious awards the film has already garnered. The producer and director, Kaveeta and Pavan Kaul, have taken the film to over thirty film festivals around the world, at which it has received a great many awards, including best film, best director, best musical score (for Swami Kriyananda's music), best cinematography, and best script.

The true power of the film, however, lies beyond all the accolades, in the inspiration that it offers and the devotion it awakens. This film has the power to bring many people onto the spiritual path, and to deepen the discipleship of those who already follow a guru. As the name implies, the answers to our problems begin to emerge when we choose to align our God-given free will with the grace of a great soul like Yoganandaji.

The world is stumbling now, lurching through a maze built of self-centeredness and greed. We will not find a way out of this darkness alone. Urgently needed is someone with a torch of wisdom to lead the way. If this film can shine a light into the world at such a time, it will be a great gift to mankind.

In the light,
NAYASWAMI JYOTISH

P.S. Rajinikanth's testimonial can be viewed at joyiswith.in/13.

GOD'S BOATMAN

We were sitting in the radiant, late-August sunlight at the Ananda Retreat, overlooking the gently rolling Umbrian hills outside of Assisi, Italy, chatting with a friend of ours from Rome. She told us with joy in her warm, brown eyes and a sweet smile on her lips, "I recently came to the Retreat feeling quite depressed about many aspects of my life. But after being here for only three days, my thoughts now are filled with such peace, and my problems all seem so trivial."

Ananda Assisi is a place of deep spiritual vibrations that heal the heart and mind as they uplift the soul. People come here from all over Europe to learn and practice Paramhansa Yogananda's teachings, but mainly to bring joy back into their lives.

Jyotish and I at the Ananda Retreat in Assisi, Italy.

Jyotish and I have been here for two weeks now, offering classes and satsangs for the guests and community members, and deeply enjoying the peace and blessedness that permeates this place. Last Saturday night we helped lead a Kriya Initiation for two hundred people coming from ten different countries. As you can imagine, a variety of languages were represented in the softly lit temple, made especially beautiful that night for the initiation. Throughout the ceremony you could hear the whisperings of

several translators helping everyone to receive Kriya in their mother tongue.

This gathering of disciples, all dressed in white and filled with a shared devotion for God and Guru, was like a vision of the future: a time when this planet will be united in peace and world brotherhood. Our guru spoke of such a time to come. As harbingers of a united world, our Kriya Masters are bringing their blessings for global upliftment.

The next day, following the Sunday Satsang and lunch, we signed copies of our new book of blogs, *Un Tocco di Gioia* (A Touch of Joy), that has come out recently in Italian. Learning people's names and signing their books gave us an opportunity personally to meet many of the devotees who had received Kriya the night before, as well as some of the other guests who were also present that day.

I kept a mental tally of all the different countries from which the people we met had come: Albania, Bulgaria, Croatia, Russia, Siberia, Australia, New Zealand, Denmark, Holland, and, of course, from all over Italy. We signed books for nearly two hours, though the time flew quickly by as we met our spiritual brothers and sisters, and they shared about their lives.

We came to understand how many had come from difficult circumstances, either nationally or personally, with health, family, or financial challenges. Yet Yoganandaji had found all of them and had changed their lives. Eyes filled with light and strength, person after person spoke of the joy of coming to Ananda and practicing Master's teachings.

My heart began to expand and soar as I felt the limitless scope of Yoganandaji's presence throughout the world, and the blessings that he brings to "all those waiting, thirsty ones."

He describes it best in his poem, "God's Boatman":

I want to ply my boat, many times,
Across the gulf after death,
And return to earth's shores
From my home in space.
I want to load my boat
With all those waiting, thirsty ones
Who have been left behind,
That I may carry them to the opalescent pool
Of iridescent joy,
There where my Father distributes
His all-desire-quenching, liquid peace.
Oh! I will come back again and again!
Crossing a million crags of suffering,
With bleeding feet, I will come,
If need be, a trillion times,
As long as I know that
One stray brother is left behind.

So, my dear friend, have no fear, for "God's Boatman" is ever seeking to find those who, from their heart, call out for God.

In His love,

NAYASWAMI DEVI

88
Sept. 6, 2018

FROM NOWHERE
to NOW HERE

Generally, insights are proceeded by a certain train of thought. But once in a while they just plop into the mind like a raindrop falling from a clear sky. Yesterday, while meditating with the Ananda Assisi community, a perception popped into my mind without any preamble: "We need to move from 'Nowhere' to 'Now Here.'" Plop!

Linguistically, it is fun—you just move a single letter to the left, which cancels the negating "no" and changes it into a positive "now." The extra space allows "nowhere" to become "now here." But what is easy to do with letters is harder to do with thoughts and emotions. How do we cancel our negative thoughts, create a little space for ourselves, and learn to live in the here and now? This, in itself, is a spiritual path.

When I first came on the spiritual path, a book called *Be Here Now*, by Ram Dass, was very popular. Its title sums up its message. Almost all paths and meditation techniques urge the practitioner to be focused in the present moment.

What is "nowhere"? It is the unsubstantial mental territory located in the nether regions of our consciousness. Fears, regrets, vague thoughts about the past and future, and other nasty creatures dwell there.

The problems of the past can continue only in this nowhere land of your own mind. It is you, only you, who nurture them even though they continue to haunt you. Paramhansa Yogananda said, "Your memory will do exactly what you tell it to do, so be careful that you do not let it repeat any unpleasant experience. . . . Remember, in your consciousness there are all kinds of records, both good and bad. You must destroy all records that revive memories of unhappiness and evil deeds and unkindness. You must scatter them to the winds."

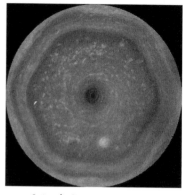

*Saturn's Streaming Hexagon.
Source: NASA/JPL-Caltech/SSI/
Hampton University.*

Likewise, you create your own bucket of worries about the future. A friend told us that his mother had fretted about a potential problem for two weeks. When it never came to pass, she had the good grace to say, "Well, I wasted a good worry on that one." Your worries, too, exist only in the nowhere land of your mind. The quickest way to overcome fear and worry is to take a few deep breaths and move your thoughts from Nowhere to Now Here.

We saw a talk by a very successful entrepreneur who was asked, "What is the secret of your success?" We loved his reply: "I am a visionary and have a very clear picture of the future. Unfortunately, my vision only extends for the next fifteen minutes. The rest of my success is due to hard work and perseverance." And so it is with the spiritual path.

People enjoy any pursuit that keeps them in the here and now. Creative pursuits—playing music, painting, cooking something new—are wonderful ways to live in the present. Play is another way and is important not only for people but for animals too. A friend sent us a delightful video of a bird playing on a sprinkler. (We've included it at the end for your amusement.) Although the video is quite short, she said the bird continued playing this way for a full five minutes!

God exists completely in the present, beyond the twin delusions of time and space, and making the shift from Nowhere to Now Here brings us closer to Him. Yogananda wrote, "When storms of trials shriek, and when worries howl at me, I will drown their noises, loudly chanting: 'God! God! God!'"

So, when your mind drifts and begins to cause you distress, bring it back immediately. Let your mantra be, "I need to move from Nowhere to Now Here."

In joy,
NAYASWAMI JYOTISH

P.S. Video of bird playing: <u>joyiswith.in/14</u>.

89
Sept. 13, 2018

WHAT'S LEFT?

Recently while in Assisi, we watched a film called "St. Giuseppe Moscati: Doctor to the Poor," which was written and directed by a good friend and fellow disciple, Giacomo Campiotti. Watching the film some years earlier, Swami Kriyananda had said it was the best spiritual movie he'd ever seen. We certainly agree.

The movie opens in 1903 in Naples, Italy, where Giuseppe Moscati begins his career as a brilliant young doctor and medical researcher. But he is also a man of great compassion, and unceasingly gives of himself to alleviate the suffering of others, especially the struggling poor. Then miracles begin to happen: People are healed of incurable diseases, sometimes just by thinking of him; or someone who was pronounced dead by the other doctors returns to life through his help.

After working long hours in the noisy, overcrowded "Hospital for the Incurable," he returns home each evening to the comfortable family home he shares with his sister. One day as he makes his rounds, a dying, abandoned woman grasps his hand and begs, "I'm afraid. Please don't let me die here."

Without hesitation, he carries her to his own home, where she quietly dies at peace. The word begins to get out among the poor, and the next morning his home is filled with penniless people begging for his medical help. From then on, every evening after he finishes his rounds, he returns home to treat all those who are waiting there.

He takes no money from these patients, but instead often gives a few lira to pay for their prescription. Eventually he is left penniless and is forced to sell even his own possessions in order to serve others. Giuseppe Moscati died peacefully in 1927 at the age of forty-seven, and in 1987 was declared a saint by the Catholic Church. Without sentimentality, the movie portrays the increasing beauty of a soul who continued to give everything of himself until all that was left was God's love.

St. Giuseppe Moscati, doctor to the poor.

His story reminded me (in a very small and humble way) of an episode with Swami Kriyananda that took place in my own life. In the early 1970s, I was on the staff at Ananda's Meditation Retreat in Northern California. In those days (brace yourself) not only did we not have computers to register guests, we didn't even have a phone. As you can imagine, we never really knew who was coming or when.

Sometimes guests would arrive with their own tents and sleeping bags, but often we would need to find an unused tent for them, or a sleeping bag from the small supply of extras we kept on hand.

On this particular Friday evening, I had already registered an unusually large number of guests, and had given out all the tents and sleeping bags we had. Since it was getting late, I was preparing to lock the office and go home to my small camper. At that moment another guest arrived, empty-handed. Not knowing what else to do, I asked him to wait a few minutes, and ran home to collect my own sleeping bag and foam pad for him. I spent a chilly night on a hard, wooden bed covered only by a thin sheet.

The next morning, as I was opening up the office, Swami Kriyananda walked in and, presumably not knowing what had happened the night before, said with a big smile, "Now you're getting the idea." No preamble, no explanation, just those words.

The other day we were talking with some friends about what we can do to dissolve the ego. Swamiji described the ego as a "bundle of self-definitions": definitions such as, "This is *my* home, *my* time, *my* space, *my* body, *my* ideas, *my* sleeping bag. . . ." As, thread by thread, we cut through the thick rope of limited self-awareness which binds this bundle together—a rope consisting of innumerable thoughts of "mine, mine, mine"—we can eventually release all the little attachments from which it's formed. Then what's left? God alone.

After our discussion a friend of ours, Sabine, in Assisi wrote this beautiful poem:

> Imagine
> You write, but the page
> stays empty.
> Imagine
> You paint and the paper
> keeps white.
> Imagine
> The pen does not cooperate,
> because the colors
> dance in the Light.

With divine friendship,
NAYASWAMI DEVI

90
Sept. 20, 2018

KEEPING IT SIMPLE

We are on the move again. We will have slept in four different hotels in the last week. Moreover, the maximum weight for flying in India is 15 kilograms (33 pounds). That's the limit of our portable possessions these days. Being a New Age wandering sadhu imposes a forced simplicity, a paring down to the essentials. That is a good thing for a yogi.

One of the most memorable quotes of Paramhansa Yogananda is, "Simplicity of living plus high thinking lead to the greatest happiness." Real simplicity is the voluntary renunciation of attachments. It's not doing without material goods—there are billions of people worldwide who live in abject poverty, which we see daily in the work Ananda does with the widows in Brindaban, India. But *voluntarily* transferring one's yearnings from the things of the world to the desire for God is quite different. This frees the heart and mind.

The essence of the spiritual path is to overcome the instinctual compulsions that surround and protect the ego. This cannot be done except by willing, enthusiastic surrender of everything that you think you own and all that you think you are. The ego tells us that this is madness, that it will end in misery. The soul and the guru, however, silently cheer us on.

How do we achieve simplicity? The first and obvious thing is to get rid of the unnecessary "necessities." Look at each of your possessions and ask these two questions: "Do I use it? Do I love it?" If the answer to both of them is "no," then it is probably old baggage taking up space in your closet and your heart. Give these things to others who actually need them and keep paring down until you feel a sense of freedom not only from your possessions but, more importantly, from the *need* to possess.

We arrive at Ananda Mumbai.

Simplicity of being is harder to achieve than the minimization of owning. And yet, the process is similar. First you must be calm and centered enough to begin to observe your "bundle of self-definitions." Then ask the same two questions in a slightly varied form: "Do I need and use this self-definition? Do I love it because it is leading me to freedom?" This allows you to drop those darkening qualities: pride, negativity, jealousy, anger, doubt—the numberless soldiers of the army of the materialist Kaurava clan of the Gita.

And it allows you to focus on supporting the few useful soul-qualities represented by the Pandavas: the ability to avoid evil, the ability to do what is right, fiery self-control, pranayama, and expansion. These plus devotion to God and Guru are all one really needs.

The life of a wandering sadhu, where you surrender the need to control your circumstances, is good for the soul. A friend summed it up this way: "Life becomes very simple. There isn't much that I do except serve and meditate." If our goal is freedom, what else do we need?

In joyful simplicity,
NAYASWAMI JYOTISH

91
Sept. 27, 2018

The WELL, the BUCKET, and the ROPE

She was a poor cleaning woman working in a hospital in Chennai, India, where a friend of ours also worked as a doctor. There was something about her that awakened compassion in our friend's heart, and a desire to help. Perhaps it was because the lady seemed so alone in the world and had a small child to raise; whatever the reasons, our friend felt strongly that she should aid her.

And so she would often bring to the hospital clothes or extra food for the woman, and tried in whatever ways she could to offer her assistance. From time to time our friend would also invite her to her home for tea, but, probably on account of the social distance between them, the woman always humbly declined.

Five years had passed in this way, when finally the woman accepted the invitation to join our friends—the doctor and her husband—for tea. As she entered their home, she saw a large photo of Paramhansa Yogananda, which hung in their living room, and burst into tears.

"Do you know who this is?" they gently asked her. Quietly nodding her head, she finally replied, "Five years ago my husband died. The day before his passing, he gave me a copy of *Autobiography of a Yogi*, and said, 'Now he will take care of you.' I have not read the book, but have kept it with me."

And so it was that Yoganandaji did take care of her through the agency of our friends. Unbeknownst to them, they had been instru-

Paramhansa Yogananda and Anandamayi Ma.

ments of his grace which helped and supported her. What brought such divine grace into this poor woman's life? Perhaps it was her deep, heartfelt prayers to God that drew it, and then manifested in our friends' desire to help her.

Recently I read a beautiful statement from the great woman saint, Anandamayi Ma, about what it is that draws grace into our lives. She said that people are mistaken when they think that grace is something that happens only occasionally or randomly. Like the child who forgets his mother when absorbed in play, we, too, in our absorption in this world, forget that Divine Mother is always aware of our needs and tends to them when the time is right.

But when we are able to dwell in steady remembrance of God, then we become more keenly aware of the constant flow of divine grace. Ma used the analogy of a well, a bucket, and a rope. The water in the well is like God's blessings, which are always freely available. The bucket can carry these blessings, but it is the rope of our constant remembrance that draws them to us.

Fortunately for us, God's grace can come to us even when we forget Him. But it is so much sweeter and richer when we remember the source. Like the poor woman who clung to Yoganandaji for protection, may we draw to us the overflowing bucket of divine grace, using the rope we have woven from our constant thought of God.

With love and joy,
NAYASWAMI DEVI

An EXULTATION *of* MUSIC

It was one of the most remarkable evenings of my life. I sat mesmerized, along with nearly two thousand five hundred others in the auditorium, listening to ragas played by some of India's finest musicians. Shiv Kumar Sharma and Hari Prasad Chaurasia have spent a lifetime mastering Indian classical music and have been awarded the highest honors of a grateful nation.

Indians will be well aware of their names and reputations, but for those from the West who haven't heard their movie soundtracks or albums, perhaps a little introduction is needed. Shiv Kumar plays the santoor, an instrument with a hundred strings and a unique sound, played as a percussion instrument with small wooden hammers, a little like a blend between a sitar and a hammered dulcimer. But, to quote P.G. Wodehouse, that is like "describing the Taj Mahal as a pretty nifty tomb."

Hari Prasad plays the Indian wooden flute. When hearing him, one begins to appreciate why Lord Krishna is depicted as entrancing devotees with his flute. They were accompanied by Vijay Ghate on tabla and Bhawani Shankar on the pakhawaj, a large, barrel-shaped wooden drum. They, too, are famous musicians, and the four of them often play together. In fact, Shiv and Hari are lifelong friends and have played together for sixty-one years.

In his introduction to the evening, Shiv Kumar said that Indian classical music and Indian spirituality are two sides of the same coin. The next morning, as we sat together with them at breakfast, Shiv said that he had read *Autobiography of a Yogi* many times, and felt that the concert's special magic was all due to the guru's grace. The concert was dedicated to Yoganandaji, this being the 125th anniversary of his birth, and was a fundraising event for the Paramhansa Yogananda Charitable Trust, which serves many thousands of widows in Brindaban, India.

In his *Autobiography* Paramhansa Yogananda says, "In India, music as well as painting and the drama is considered a divine art. Brahma, Vishnu, and Shiva—the Eternal Trinity—were the first musicians. The Divine Dancer Shiva is scripturally represented as having worked out the infinite modes of rhythm in His cosmic dance of universal creation." The ragas have a power to bring one's energy inward and upward and to connect one to God.

The duet between the santoor and the flute, going back and forth with increasing complexity and intensity, seemed like a dialogue in heaven. Add to this the tabla and pakhawaj and it felt like a conversation among four Gods, who were talking, laughing, teasing, competing, and uplifting one another in a language that bypassed the mind and went straight to the heart and soul.

The whole purpose of the spiritual path is to raise the consciousness, drawing it inward and upward, dissolving the separation of ego. Absorption in whatever we love leads to losing our sense of isolation and merging with a greater reality. Meditation is one way of doing this; so also is the divine art of uplifted music.

Try it for yourself by watching a video of the concert. (The link is below.) I suggest that you listen in a setting where

you can be silent and inward. I would even recommend that you use earphones and prepare to sit in silence after the music finishes. I think you will be transported to a higher realm. Devi and I, along with all of the others in the concert hall, certainly were.

In the eternal AUM,
NAYASWAMI JYOTISH

P.S. You can watch the concert at joyiswith.in/1.

INTEGRITY vs. SHOWMANSHIP

Swami Kriyananda sat with his eyes closed and a blissful smile on his face as he listened to a piece of music by Wolfgang Amadeus Mozart. As it ended, Swamiji quietly remarked, "Mozart was a consummate artist. He never compromised integrity for showmanship."

I reflected for quite some time on Swamiji's words, trying to understand their subtlety and depth. What I finally concluded he meant was that Mozart never took the well-trodden path of "playing to the crowd" to achieve popularity or success. Rather he chose to express in his music personal honesty, as well as a timeless truth and beauty. This is what touches the heart of every sensitive listener, and why Mozart's compositions are still widely appreciated hundreds of years later.

This same integrity is found equally in Swami Kriyananda's own music and writing. He once said that he never intruded a single note of music, or a single word in his books, that wasn't absolutely sincere. What a powerful thought. And what a spiritual guideline for our own life!

Swami Kriyananda once said that he never intruded a single note of music, or a single word in his books, that wasn't absolutely sincere.

For we too must become "consummate artists" in whatever role God has given us, a role determined by the karmic lessons we need to learn. The prince or the print maker, the rock star or the stonemason—in God's eyes no part is better or more important than another. What is important is to live with as much sincerity and personal integrity as possible. Try to replace the thought, "Will this win me acceptance, praise, or popularity?" with "Is this pleasing to God and my own higher Self?"

Each day will present its own challenges and difficulties. Step back from the daily fray, and inwardly listen to God's inner guidance. The details may vary, but the essence will invariably be: Be true to yourself. Seek to please Me in all things. Find joy in every situation, even in the seeming setbacks. Accept whatever comes with a sense of purpose and poise.

Finally, remember this prayer of Paramhansa Yogananda: "Beloved Father, I realize that praise does not make me any better, nor blame worse. I am what I am before my conscience and Thee. I shall travel on, doing good to all and seeking ever to please Thee, for thus shall I find my only true happiness."

In divine friendship,
NAYASWAMI DEVI

The POWER of a POSITIVE MIND

We recently attended a program by an Indian doctor on the power of the mind. Some years ago he was dying of cancer, was given only a few days to live. Then he had an experience of God telling him he would be healed through the power of his mind. In his case, God had to come three times to reassure him, since his thoughts kept slipping back into doubt and hopelessness. He was completely cured and has dedicated himself to helping others do the same.

Sri Yukteswar, guru of Paramhansa Yogananda, author of Autobiography of a Yogi.

His premise is that all illness is psychosomatic, meaning that it has both a mental (psyche) and physical (somatic) component. Our thoughts and emotions affect the body through various chemical, electrical, and hormonal pathways. But most healing modalities completely ignore the importance of the mind and emotions and therefore never address a disease's root cause. He used this example: Suppose your air conditioner (or an internal organ) is not functioning well. If the cause of the problem is a lack of energy going through the wires, it will not matter how many parts you replace. The answer is to fix the wiring (mental) system, which in turn is connected to the divine power source. This is done by training ourselves to direct the mind to avoid negative thoughts and emotions and replace them with positive ones.

This is entirely in keeping with the teachings of Paramhansa Yogananda, who often spoke about the immense power of the positive, God-attuned mind. When we tune in to God, through meditation or other forms of sadhana, and turn on the switch of positivity, His intelligent life-force flows through us to heal, inspire, magnetize, and transform us.

There are many examples of this in *Autobiography of a Yogi*. One of the most remarkable was the time when Sri Yukteswar's health improved and declined dramatically according to the suggestions of his guru, Lahiri Mahasaya. In the end Lahiri said, "Really, it has been your thoughts that have made you feel alternately weak and strong. You have seen how your health has exactly followed your expectations. Thought is a force, even as electricity or gravitation. The human mind is a spark of the almighty consciousness of God. I could show you that whatever your powerful mind believes very intensely would instantly come to pass."

How can we control our thoughts and emotions? The first step is to be able to focus the mind. This can be enabled especially by meditation, visualization, and controlling the breath. Once we learn to focus the mind, the next step is simply to tell it to focus intensely on what we want. A light bulb sends out rays in all directions, but the focused beam of a flashlight can be moved from one object to another at our choosing.

When a negative thought enters the mind, immediately stop it from gathering momentum. You can do this by clearly visualizing an image for two or three minutes in as much detail as possible. The mind is now focused and ready for you to aim it toward a positive quality counteractive to that negative thought. This two-step technique for replacing negative thoughts and feelings with positive ones is not that hard to do, but it takes resolve to overcome old habit patterns that prevent us from *trying*.

It is worth the struggle, however, for a positive mind is the key to health, happiness, and our constant connection to the Divine within.

In joy,
NAYASWAMI JYOTISH

95
Oct. 25, 2018

QUIT COUNTING!

I'm a people watcher: I love observing people as they go about their business. I try to see what their faces and body language reveal, and then imagine what they're like and what kind of lives they lead.

One thing I often observe is the restless movements people make while they're waiting—to board a plane, for example, or for someone to join them in a hotel lobby. The nervous drumming of fingers, tapping of feet, and glancing at cell phones ("mobiles" here in India) are common sights in the frenetic age in which we live.

What is happening to our consciousness when we live in such a restless way? Repetitive, nervous movements of the body, eyes, and especially, the mind break up our experience of reality and time into small, discrete units. When we measure it in quick little beats, life itself becomes fragmented and disjointed.

I had an unusual experience as I was finishing my senior year of college just a few weeks before I moved to Ananda. It was a beautiful spring day, and I decided to go for a walk along a large lake that bordered the campus. After a while I sat and gazed at the variety of activities before me: people picnicking and laughing together; families of ducks paddling and quacking boisterously; swimmers gracefully moving through the water; sailboats gliding swiftly over the surface; trees swaying in the breeze; billowy clouds; sunlight sparkling on the water.

Then, like the unexpected emergence of a hidden image in an optical illusion, my perception suddenly changed. Instead of many separate objects in the scene before me, I saw only one thing—an undivided whole. The thought arose in my mind, "How did anyone ever conceive of the number one, for there are no separate parts to be counted?" (Interestingly, the mathematical concept of zero originated in India.) This perception had a profound and lasting effect on me.

Shortly afterwards I found a passage in Paramhansa Yogananda's *Autobiography of a Yogi* that helped me understand my experience. In an explanation of *maya*, the literal meaning of which is "the measurer," he wrote: "Maya is the magical power in creation by which limitations and divisions are apparently present in the Immeasurable and Inseparable." As I was about to devote myself to a spiritual search, I was given a glimpse of the "immeasurable and inseparable" nature of reality.

Here are some tips to help you to stop measuring the "immeasurable," or, to put it simply, to quit counting the pieces and look at the whole.

In Daily Life:

> 1. Whatever your circumstances, good or bad, don't think about how many days or weeks before it's over. When on vacation, don't think, "Only one week left," but enjoy what experiences come to you each day. When going through a stressful workweek, don't project, "In two days I can rest." Rather put out the energy that is required to finish the job.

> 2. When you're with friends or family, train your mind to be fully present, and don't dwell on thoughts like, "I have to leave in five minutes," or, "I have three phone calls to make, so I'd better speed this up."

> 3. When you begin each day, take stock of what needs to be done, then try to see your activities as a flow rather than as separate events. You'll have much more energy if you see each day as a whole—supported by an underlying enthusiasm for life.

In Meditation:

1. Swami Kriyananda said, "Train yourself not to move a muscle." When you begin your meditation, close your eyes, and keep them closed until you're finished. Don't look at your watch to see how long you've meditated, or how much time is left.

Relax your body and mind, and enjoy the peace.

2. If you're meditating in a group, the leader will end it at the appropriate time. Relax your body and mind, and enjoy the peace.

3. If you're meditating alone, there are two options. If you need to finish at a certain time, you can set a quiet alarm to go off at the right moment. If you have no time constraints, do your techniques and practice devotion for as long as you enjoy it.

Finally, try to live in the longer rhythms of life, in remembrance of the "immeasurable and inseparable." As Swami Kriyananda says in one of his songs:

> There's joy all around us!
> Why wait till tomorrow?
> We've only this moment to live.

May your every moment be filled with eternal joy.
NAYASWAMI DEVI

FIVE QUICK STRESS BREAKERS

"I'm feeling so stressed at work. What can I do about it?"

This, or a variation, is one of the questions we hear most often as we travel and share with others. Recently we gave a talk on "Finding Inner Peace in a Stressful World." I will give five quick techniques for dealing with stress, but first let's look quickly at both its positive and negative aspects.

We need some stress in order to flourish. Luther Burbank, the great botanist and saint, found something amazing in working with plants. In order to develop new qualities, plants need to be stressed. For instance, a sun-loving plant moved into the shade will develop a stronger stem and larger leaves. Burbank said that when stressed, a plant goes back into its genetic history to find new expressions. Weightlifters know that they must push a muscle to failure in order for it to grow stronger.

But too much stress, especially when chronic, is dangerous. Stress pushes us into the fight-or-flight syndrome, which releases a flood of chemicals and hormones into the body. This is useful for dealing

Tulips at Crystal Hermitage Gardens.
Photo by Barbara Bingham.

with an unexpected threat, like spotting a cobra near your door. (I use this illustration because we actually did see a cobra outside of our door at a retreat near Bangalore a few days ago. Before you gasp and feel a flood of second-hand stress, it was only a baby, about a foot long, and was being gently herded toward a safe area by a guard with a broom.)

But, back to stress. Many people find themselves in high-pressure situations at work or at home, where neither fight nor flight is appropriate. If we realize that most of the stress we feel comes from inside, from our reactive process, then we have found something we can work with. Here are five quick solutions. For fun, I've also listed the approximate time needed for each.

1. Breathe. Have a little tool kit of breathing techniques at your disposal. Just taking five deep breaths will help. Even better is to do a few rounds of the simple pranayama "regular breathing": inhale slowly for a count of eight, hold eight, and exhale for a count of eight. The length of the breath can vary according to what is comfortable, but make sure the counts are all the same. Yogananda recommended that we do this daily while walking, but it can also be used in any stressful situation. Approximate time: one minute.

2. Mentally recast the situation. A well-known story illustrates this method: Imagine being on a crowded bus about to sip coffee from your cup, when someone jostles your arm, spilling the hot liquid all over you. As you are about to give him a piece of your mind, you see that he is blind. Immediately compassion rises and your stress level drops. Everyone is blind in their own way. If you recast a stressful situation, you get back into control. Time: one minute.

3. Change your focus. When confronted with your own stress producers — negative moods or thoughts — break their momentum by visualizing a pleasant scene very clearly for one or two minutes. Then, with your mind diverted, you can refocus it on a positive thought or mood. Time: two minutes.

4. Bring your energy to the spiritual eye. Press your forefinger at the spiritual eye briefly while deeply concentrating there, trying to see light and feel joy. Time: thirty seconds.

5. Practice gratitude. Everything that happens is an expression of God's love and His desire for our freedom. Whatever comes, say, "Thank you, God. Thank you, God. Thank you, God." And mean it. Time: five seconds or a lifetime.

Total time for all five quick stress breakers: 4 minutes, 35 seconds.

The best stress buster of all is meditation, but that is better left to another blog.

In peace and joy,
NAYASWAMI JYOTISH

97
Nov. 8, 2018

JUST DO IT

"Master wants you to lecture in his place at the San Diego temple this weekend. . . . He also wants you to give a Kriya Yoga Initiation afterwards." These words were delivered to Swami Kriyananda (then James Donald Walters) after he had been with his guru, Paramhansa Yogananda, for only a few months.

His reaction was both disbelief and shock. "But," he sputtered to the monk conveying his guru's instructions, "everyone there is expecting Master to give the lecture after his absence of over three months. Besides, I'm only twenty-two years old, I've never spoken in public, and I've only been to one Kriya Initiation myself."

"Well," the brother monk replied, "he wants you to go. Here's some money for the bus. You'd better leave immediately."

The terrified young "Walter" did take the next bus, and was an inspiring representative for his guru that day. Thus began Swami Kriyananda's life as a spiritual teacher, one that spanned the next

Nitai with the elementary school children. Learn more about Education for Life at edforlife.org.

sixty-five years and brought Yoganandaji's teachings to millions around the world.

Beyond its significance in Swamiji's own life, this incident also contains a lesson for all of us. Kriyananda did what was asked of him, even though his guru's request seemed far beyond his level of experience or self-definition at that time. By doing it, he transcended the contractive ego that draws a line in the sand and says, "This is who I am, and this is what I can do." A better attitude for a devotee to hold is, "I'm not going to limit who I am, or what I'm really capable of." This leaves more room for spiritual growth.

Yoganandaji didn't carefully define what he wanted Swamiji to say at the lecture, or how he was to give the initiation, but rather empowered and guided him from within. It's a story we've seen repeated many times in Ananda's history.

Nitai, who had been a school teacher before coming to the community, once commented to Swamiji, "Many families with children are starting to move to Ananda. We really need a school here to serve them."

"You're right," Kriyananda replied. "Can you start one based on Master's principles of education?"

"But," said Nitai with some bewilderment, "I've never seen these principles, and I've never started a school."

"Well, read whatever you can find, and do your best," was Swamiji's reply.

Nitai did as he'd been asked, and for the next ten years helped create an innovative system of education reflecting Yoganandaji's methods of training children on all levels, body, mind, and spirit. Only after the school was well established did Swami Kriyananda write his book, *Education for Life*. In it, he created a handbook for Ananda's "Living Wisdom Schools," in which he described in more detail the theory and practice upon which that school, and others that were to be founded in later years, are based.

True spiritual guides like Yoganandaji, and later, in his turn, Kriyanandaji, when assigning someone a task, don't specify in detail what they want done, or closely direct every action. They have the wisdom to know that it is as a devotee tunes in himself to higher guidance that understanding, growth, and attunement come.

Remember this principle when you are asked by someone you respect, or by your own higher Self, to take on a challenge that seems beyond your present capacity or self-conception. If you doubt your ability to fulfill the task, believe that God can do it through you. By just trying, we can become channels for divine consciousness, and thus move toward greater self-awareness and freedom.

With joy in the doing,
NAYASWAMI DEVI

98
Nov. 15, 2018

HOW to MAKE BETTER DECISIONS

Making good decisions is one of life's most important skills, and yet we have gotten virtually no training. Sometimes even life-defining choices such as marriage, job, or taking up a spiritual quest are given little energy. Here is an illuminating example.

Some years ago, in India, we had dinner with a fine, noble man who once had been a doctor. One weekend two friends told him they were going to take an extremely competitive exam to qualify for high-level civil service jobs. If successful, they would be assured a life with financial security and high status. Over a million would be taking the test, and they had been preparing for months. Almost jokingly they invited our doctor friend to come along. You can probably guess the result—only he passed the exam. When we met him years later, and he recounted the story, he held the important job of planning traffic patterns for the whole Delhi area and was, indeed, financially secure and highly respected. He was also desperately unfulfilled. On a whim, he had abandoned his original calling.

Have you ever met someone who, like him, found themselves on a sort of karmic bullet train taking them for a ride that they never really asked for, let alone consciously directed? Maybe this has even happened to you. Here are the ways we usually make decisions, and how we can improve.

1. Subconscious, habit-driven, impulsive decisions. Many daily choices, and some critical ones, are made by subconscious impulse. They just seem to happen, and only later do we become aware of the ramifications. The cure: Get clear about your life goals. Swami Kriyananda wrote, "Life is a quest for inner joy." If that is a life goal for you, then evaluate the decisions you make, large and small, to see where they are leading you.

2. Conscious decisions directed by reason. Conscious decisions are often made with a lot of thought and worry. The difficulty is that they are limited by the degree of wisdom we do or don't have. The cure: Ask for guidance. Yogananda said to pray this way: "I will reason, I will will, I will act, but guide Thou my reason, will, and activity to the right path in everything." You can also ask for clarity from a wise and trusted friend.

3. Semi-intuitive guidance. These are the gut feelings you might have, based mainly on feeling and experience. In most cases you should trust your instincts, but check them against your reason and common sense.

4. Superconscious intuition. This comes with stillness of mind and heart and a deep desire to attune your individual will with God. For important decisions it's good to get away from your normal environment. Take seclusion in an uplifted place. Let your mind calm down, and then meditate deeply. Float your question into the light, feeling that you are an empty vessel ready to receive divine guidance. In deep stillness you can hear God's whispers, which

Float your question into the light, feeling that you are an empty vessel ready to receive divine guidance.

might come as a lucidly clear thought or as a deep, calm knowing in your heart.

When you live your life in attunement with higher consciousness, your decisions will always lead you toward your life's true goals.

In divine friendship,
NAYASWAMI JYOTISH

99
Nov. 22, 2018

LESSONS LEARNED

Recently in Mumbai, India, we were asked the question: "What are some of the lessons you've learned on your spiritual journey, especially those involving Swami Kriyananda?" I'd like to share some of my responses with you, because they touch on issues that each of us faces as a devotee.

Lesson #1:
Does God Really Know That
I'm Making a Spiritual Effort?

When we're new at meditation and not sure of what we're doing, it's easy to fall into the trap of feeling inadequate yet unsupported in our efforts. We may ask ourselves, "Does God even know I'm here, or that I'm trying?"

I want to assure you that at many points along my journey, I've been shown that no spiritual effort goes unnoticed, and that God has been cheering us on all along the way. For example, in the second year that I was at Ananda, I was living at the Meditation Retreat in a small trailer that was nestled in a quiet wooded glen. I was doing my best to meditate regularly, but often my meditations were, let's say, less than stellar.

One morning, however, I had a breakthrough and enjoyed a deep, still period of meditation. Afterwards, as I was walking along the forest path to the dining room for breakfast, I saw Swami Kriyananda talking with a group of people some distance away. Although his back was towards me, and he was about one hundred yards away, as I drew closer, he abruptly turned, left the group, and walked over to me.

Taking my hands in his and looking deeply into my eyes, Swamiji quietly said, "Very good." That was all.

Stunned, I thought, "He knew!" This experience, and others like it, gave me assurance that the Divine Eye *is* watching. God, through wise teachers, is cheering us on in our achievements, and encouraging us despite our failures.

Lesson #2:
Am I Making Any Spiritual Progress?

Swami Kriyananda gave more and more of himself until every act was offered to God.

Once Jyotish and I were riding in a car with Swamiji, and he was discussing how well some Ananda members were doing spiritually. I wasn't trying to focus the discussion on my own life, but almost inadvertently I said, "I don't know that I've really changed all that much in the years I've been on the path."

With a great deal of energy, he responded, "How can you say that? You're an entirely different person than when you came." Swamiji went on to say that it's very difficult to see changes in ourselves, because what falls away isn't who we ever were anyway. Rather, as we progress spiritually we come to dwell more in our own soul nature, which is so familiar that we often aren't aware of it. The ability to remain calm and joyful in all of life's circumstances is often a truer sign of spiritual progress than even experiences or visions in meditation.

Lesson #3:
What Is the Best Way to Make a Life Commitment to Your Spiritual Goals?

The example of Swami Kriyananda's own life was the best teacher for this lesson. As the years went by, he gave more and more of himself until there wasn't a drop of blood, a breath, a spoken or written word, a musical note, or an act of service to others that hadn't been offered. To stay the course and remain on the spiritual path for a lifetime means increased self-offering every step of the way.

At first, we're asked to give very little. But as time goes by, we're asked to give more and more of ourselves — of our service, our time and energy, our thoughts, and our love. Eventually we realize that the more we give, the more strength we have to continue the journey to the end.

With love in God and Guru,
NAYASWAMI DEVI

100
Nov. 29, 2018

SING YOUR WAY
to FREEDOM

We recently read a story about Pete Seeger, the well-known singer and social activist. Many of his songs became themes for social justice, environmental awareness, and non-violence. Here is the wonderful story:

In the 1970s, Pete Seeger was invited to sing in Barcelona, Spain. Francisco Franco's fascist government, the last of the dictatorships that started World War II, was still in power, but declining. A pro-democracy movement was gaining strength, and to prove it, they invited America's best-known freedom singer to Spain. More than a hundred thousand people were in the stadium, where rock bands had played all day. But the crowd had come for Seeger.

As Pete prepared to go on, government officials handed him a list of songs he was not allowed to sing. Pete studied it mournfully, saying it looked an awful lot like his set list. But they insisted: He must not sing any of these songs.

Pete took the government's list of banned songs and strolled on stage. He held up the paper and said, "I've been told that I'm not allowed to sing these songs." He grinned at the crowd and said, "So I'll just play the chords; maybe you know the words. They didn't say anything about you singing them."

He strummed his banjo for one song after another, and they all sang: a hundred thousand defiant freedom singers breaking the law with Pete Seeger, filling the stadium with words their government did not want them to hear, words they all knew and had sung together, in secret circles, for years.

At Ananda we have learned how powerful music is as a way to change consciousness. That is why Swami Kriyananda composed more than 450 pieces, and why Paramhansa Yogananda said, "Chanting is half the battle." One of his chants has these lyrics:

> Oh life is sweet and death a dream, when Thy song flows through me.
>
> Then joy is sweet, sorrow a dream, when Thy song flows through me.
>
> Then health is sweet, sickness a dream, when Thy song flows through me.
>
> Then praise is sweet and blame a dream, when Thy song flows through me.

Be very careful about the music you listen to, and even more careful about the songs you sing, because melodies and lyrics stay in the mind to work their spell for good or ill. Fill your day with uplifting music and you will be halfway to happiness. Chant during meditation and during daily activities. Sing Swami Kriyananda's songs when you're alone and when you're with friends. (We've recently started doing sing-alongs at Ananda Village so that everyone, children and adults alike, can join voices together.)

Music is a fundamental force of creation. *Proof of Heaven*, by Eben Alexander, is one of the most powerful accounts of an after-death experience I've ever read. Dr. Alexander, a neurosurgeon, was brain-dead for more than a week. During that time he experienced a heavenly realm of incredible grace and beauty, a world that was sustained by

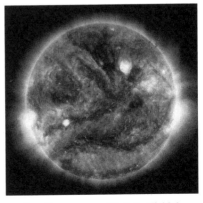

Even the sun sings. Photo by NASA.

the singing of angels much as our world is sustained by sunlight. By the way, did you know that even the sun sings? Listen to it at joyiswith.in/15.

God, you see, sings the universe into existence. When we sing in harmony with Him, we become His instruments. Let us sing beauty into existence. Let us sing of love, and peace, and joy. Let us sing ourselves all the way to spiritual freedom.

In God's song,
NAYASWAMI JYOTISH

101
Dec. 6, 2018

THANK YOU, DEAR INDIA

Usually we write our blogs with you in mind, dear friend, but this time I'm going to do something different. After nearly three months in India, we'll be returning to America in a few days. Although it will be a welcome change to stop traveling and have some familiar things around, my heart is filled with profound appreciation for all that we've received here. So, if you'd like, you're welcome to read my love letter to India.

Thank you, dear India, for the depth and beauty of your people. The light of God that shines in their eyes, their gentleness, and their subtlety have endeared them to me forever. The slightest nod of a head can communicate volumes and renders words superfluous.

Thank you, dear India, for your profusion of brilliant colors—the reds, blues, magentas, pinks, and neon greens in birds, in flowers, and in the colorful saris that even the poorest of laborers wears. You offer a vision of life in technicolor, while the rest of the world remains in stark black and white.

Thank you, dear India, for your cities, where the overwhelming abundance of life—of housewives, children, students, businessmen, merchants, cows, dogs, pigeons, pigs, and monkeys—boggles the mind until one tries to see the One Divine Life behind it all.

Thank you, dear India, for your insane traffic congestion that absorbs buses, cars, motorcycles, bicycles, and motorized

and bicycle rickshaws into a great organic being that pulses and lumbers forward, and somehow delivers everyone to where they want to go.

Thank you, dear India, for breaking my heart at the sight of homeless, ragged adults and children begging from indifferent BMW drivers; or at watching a little girl with no prospects of a better life happily performing backflips to receive a few rupees from the luxury cars that stop at the traffic light.

Thank you, dear India, for being a study of contrasts: of the mounds of filth and garbage along the street not far from high-rise offices and apartment buildings that rival the most innovative architecture in the West.

Thank you, dear India, for the intensity of your feelings, whether it be the pride and discipline of the military, the sensuality of Bollywood dancers, the vehemence of politicians, the love for children in families, or the devotion of saints seeking God.

Thank you, dear India, for the Himalayas, which never have entirely become a part of this material world. They stand as aloof, remote, and silent sentinels of a higher sphere of existence, and call to our souls to soar to their heights.

Thank you, dear India, for the friends you've given us from every part of your land. They've helped and cared for us in unimaginable ways—always available; always showing us how to solve the problems before us; always offering a meal or a cup of chai; always making us feel not like foreigners, but as cherished parts of their own family.

Thank you, dear India, for sending my Guru to America with his oceans of love, joy, and wisdom; and for allowing us to bring a tiny cupful of his gifts back to your shores.

Dear India, when my life is done, I hope that you'll receive some of my ashes to mingle with the indescribable sacredness you've given to the world.

Your child always,
NAYASWAMI DEVI

SON-BATHING

"Babaji and Christ," by Nayaswami Jyotish.

It is nearing Christmas, and next week Ananda centers will host the annual eight-hour Christmas meditation. This long meditation is a spiritual anchor for many of us, and so I thought it would be helpful to give some tips on how to deepen our meditations, especially longer ones.

In order to sit for a long period of time, or even a short one, relaxation is essential. One time Swami Kriyananda asked his guru, Paramhansa Yogananda, "Am I not trying hard enough?" Yogananda replied, "You are trying *too* hard. It is creating tension."

Effort is needed, yes, but relaxed effort. Spiritually, one of the reasons to practice yoga postures is that it teaches you to *relax* into a pose. Tensing just blocks you from going deeper. The same is true of meditation: You need to relax in order to reach the depths.

The spiritual eye in the forehead is the seat of higher consciousness, and where we will experience Christ (or Krishna) consciousness. Yogananda explained that Christ and Krishna were called "Sons of God" because they had realized their unity with God in creation. The goal of meditation is to experience this realization for ourselves. And yet, straining for it is counterproductive.

We strain because we have a latent sense that God is "out there" far away, up in the clouds, in the heavens. But the truth is that He is the air we breathe, the water we drink, the blood flowing in our veins, and the very atoms of the universe. We don't need to reach out to Him so much as to still our minds and emotions, which brings the realization that He is present already within us.

To help you relax, here is an image that came to me. When you are sun-bathing, there is no thought of trying to lift yourself up to the rays: You simply let them come to you. Try Son-bathing, then. Instead of striving mightily to lift yourself up to God, let Him come to you. Relax and bathe in the radiance of the spiritual eye. You will find that you can go deeper than if you strain.

Here are some more simple tips for deepening any meditation:

1. Start off with concentration. The first few minutes will set the tone for the rest of your meditation.

2. Practice your techniques with the deepest attention you can muster, but let that attention be relaxed.

3. Concentrate deeply, but more with the feelings than with the mind.

4. In longer meditations, your focus may wax and wane. Just be patient and keep trying. You will find that you go deeper over time.

5. Chanting is half the battle. Focus on one chant for a long period and try to take it deep. Paramhansa Yogananda spiritualized the chants by taking them into the superconscious state. Try to do the same.

6. Toward the end of each meditation try to float in a sea of joy.

May this Christmas season find you one with the Christ Consciousness.

In the One,
NAYASWAMI JYOTISH

103
Dec. 20, 2018

WHO IS *the* OTHER WISE MAN?

One of the intriguing accounts surrounding the birth of Jesus Christ is the story of the three wise men, or magi, who traveled from the East to bring him gifts of gold, and frankincense, and myrrh. Paramhansa Yogananda tells us that these three wise men were, in fact, Babaji, Lahiri Mahasaya, and Sri Yukteswar in earlier incarnations, and that later in his life Jesus traveled to India to return their visit.

One of my favorite tales told at Christmastime is called "The Story of the Other Wise Man." I'd like to share it with you as a gift, and hope that it brings you as much inspiration as it does me.

The story goes that at the time of Christ's birth there was a fourth wise man who was also watching the skies and knew that a great enlightened being was about to appear on earth. He was in communion with the other magi, and they agreed to meet at a designated spot when a special star appeared. Together then they would travel across the desert to Jerusalem, where they believed the "Son of God" would appear.

In preparation, the fourth wise man sold all of his possessions and bought three beautiful gems to offer as gifts to the Christ child: a brilliant blue sapphire, a radiant red ruby, and a pure white pearl. Finally the foretold evening arrived, and a star of heavenly power, majesty, and light appeared in the sky. Tucking his jewels carefully into his tunic, and jumping onto his horse, he took off at great speed to meet the other magi at the agreed-upon place.

The distance was great, but he and his horse journeyed determinedly on for days. Finally, with only a few hours left to reach the meeting place on time, he stopped briefly at an oasis to take some water. In the darkness, the wise man heard moaning nearby, and found an old man who lay ill. Torn between the need to press on and the desire to help, he decided to delay his onward journey briefly to aid this stranger in need.

He gave him water and healing herbs, and as the man's strength began to return, he also offered him his bread and wine. Miraculously the man recovered, and offered these unexpected words: "What you are seeking will not be found in Jerusalem, but in Bethlehem."

With great urgency the wise man made for the meeting place, only to find that the three other magi had already departed, leaving him this note: "We couldn't wait any longer. Follow us across the desert." By now, his horse was exhausted and his supplies were gone, so to continue his journey he was forced to make for a nearby town. There he reluctantly sold the sapphire to purchase camels and food for the trip through the desert to Bethlehem.

After great effort, he finally arrived on the outskirts of Bethlehem, and stopped at a small cluster of sheds. From one of the dwellings he heard the cooing of a mother and child, so he eagerly knocked on the door and was invited to enter. There he found a young mother and baby, and though they were clearly not the ones he was seeking, the mother offered him this news: "Three days ago three strangers from afar stopped at a nearby shed where Joseph of Nazareth, his wife, Mary, and their newborn son had taken refuge. They presented the child with gifts, and then disappeared. Joseph and Mary also fled the next day to escape the persecution by the Roman soldiers. Rumor has it that they went to Egypt."

The young woman kindly offered the tired stranger what little food she had. Then suddenly there was a scream from outside: "The soldiers are killing all the Jewish children!" At the sound of a loud pounding on the door, the mother clutched her child and cowered in a dark corner. Though again torn about what to do, the fourth wise man opened the door, and said to the soldier who held a sword dripping with blood, "There is no one here but me. This ruby would convince any soldier that he should move on." Greedily snatching the gem, the man strode off.

Then with unexpected insight, the young mother told him, "The king you are looking for will not be found in palaces, but among the poor, needy, and downcast."

Thus began years of searching—throughout Egypt and Israel—but never did he find what he was seeking. He did, however, find many to help: He fed the hungry, healed the sick, and comforted the rejected. Thirty-three years passed in this way, and the fourth wise man had grown worn and weary when he finally arrived in Jerusalem for the last time in search of his King.

There he found great agitation in the streets, and throngs of people surging toward something outside the city. When the weary seeker asked what was happening, he was told, "There is to be an execution on Golgotha: two thieves and a man named Jesus of Nazareth whom some call 'King of the Jews.'"

The wise man was stunned. "This must be the one I have been seeking," he thought. "Maybe I can use my last gift, the pearl, to buy his freedom." But as he began to follow the crowd up the streets to Golgotha, he heard a scream, and saw a young woman being dragged away by some soldiers. She was able to break free for a moment and run to the old wise man begging for his help. Once again overcoming his own inner conflict, he gave the soldiers the pure white pearl to buy the girl's freedom.

Then the sky darkened, lightning flashed, and the earth itself convulsed. A loosened stone fell from a building, and struck the old man on the head. Dazed, he stumbled, but the young girl caught him in her arms and lowered his head onto her lap. She looked at his worn face, and was amazed to see that suddenly it had become transfigured with light. With a far-off gaze, he said in a faint voice, "Not so, my Lord! For when did I see thee hungered, and feed thee? Or thirsty, and give thee drink? Three-and-thirty years have I looked for thee; but I have never seen thy face, nor ministered to thee, my King." Then a voice of divine power spoke, and even the young woman heard it.

Who is this fourth wise man, and what were the words he heard? In these times we see all around us hungry, displaced children, and homeless people who have lost everything. We, who are seeking Christ consciousness, are that fourth wise man. Humanity's need is great now, and we are being given the opportunity to alleviate people's suffering in many different ways. When we willingly offer compassion and comfort to others, we, too, may find what we are seeking, and hear the same words that wise man did: "Verily I say unto thee, inasmuch as thou hast done it unto one of the least of these my brethren, thou hast done it unto Me."

*May the blessings of God, Christ, and Guru
be with you in this holy season.*
NAYASWAMI DEVI

MY NEW YEAR'S RESOLUTIONS

Some years ago we were leading a New Year's retreat in which one of the exercises was to write down your resolutions for the coming year. Afterwards one of the guests came up to Devi and said, "I find that really disappointing."

"What?" she asked.

The man replied, "You've been on the path for so many years, and you still have things in yourself that you're working on."

A friend, who has a wonderful sense a humor, was observing the scene and rescued the day by saying, "Devi is the only one among us who isn't perfect. That's why we have her working with the guests."

At the peril of disillusioning you, dear friend, I thought you might enjoy seeing my New Year's resolutions for the coming year. I'll keep it simple, which suits my nature.

1. To do my best to keep my mind and heart positive and expansive. If I can get this one right, everything else will fall into place naturally. Our consciousness is like a giant funnel. As our energy moves up it expands until, ultimately, it leads to Self-realization. As it moves down, it contracts, which leads to "self-I-ness"—usually spelled with an "sh" as selfishness. The upper part of the funnel fills us with happiness, inclusiveness, and joy.

The lower part shrinks our heart and mind. This year, I want to try to keep my energy always moving upward, and nudge up the level of my specific gravity.

2. To be more actively caring and friendly. I usually try to keep my heart open and positive. When I do, I can see that light fills me and radiates outward to all those around me. For me, the most natural expression of love is as expansive friendship, kindness, and caring. This year, I want to let those qualities be more obvious, less hidden. I'll try, however, to avoid imposing on others. If I have a little light to share, it is better to offer it gently, as a way to illuminate their path ahead, than to shine it brightly in their eyes, assuming that my insight is what *they* need.

3. To be deeper in those practices that move me upward. I have all the spiritual techniques and teachings I can meaningfully use. I just have to do them more and better. With those where I'm still weak, I'll take on two at a time (one habit of meditation, and one of lifestyle) until they become permanently fixed in my daily routine.

4. To stay connected more consciously to God and Gurus throughout the day. Wanting to do this is not the problem. Remembering to do it is.

There are also a couple of things I still do that pull my energy down. I'll make an effort to avoid them.

1. Spending too much time with news and media. Over the years, the news has become less informative and more filled with gossip and judgmental opinions. I don't need to open myself to energies that seek only to stir up negative reactions.

2. **Multitasking.** Especially while I'm meditating, but also during the day. I'll try to focus on one thing at a time, to "Be Here Now."

This list is long enough. If I can accomplish or even improve on these, it will be a successful year. I offer this suggestion to you when you make your own list: Focus primarily on changing your consciousness. It is from that seed that all habits and outer behaviors grow.

May your new year be filled with light, love, and an ever-rising energy.

In joy,
NAYASWAMI JYOTISH

PHOTOGRAPHERS and ARTISTS

ii	Ananda Image Library
2	Ananda Image Library
4	Ananda Image Library
7	Ananda Image Library
9	"A Perfect Day" by Nayaswami Jyotish
11	Public Domain
12	Photo of the Yuba River by Barbara Bingham
14	"Hanalei Bay" (Hanalei, Kauai) by Nayaswami Jyotish
16	"Bee Balm." Photography by Craig P. Burrows.
19	Ananda Image Library
22	Photo by Nayaswami Jyotish
25	Ananda Image Library
27	"Eternity" by Nayaswami Jyotish
30	Photo by U.S. Air Force Senior Airman Joshua Strang
31	Ananda Image Library
35	Photo by Barbara Bingham
37	Ananda Image Library
39	Ananda Image Library
42	Ananda Image Library
45	Public Domain
47	"Mountains in the Mist" by Nayaswami Jyotish
50	Ananda Image Library
59	Public Domain
52	"The One in All" by Nayaswami Jyotish
56	Photo by Chandi Holliman
59	"The Cosmic Sea" by Nayaswami Jyotish
62	Public Domain
63	Photo by Swami Kriyananda
66	Photo by Paramhansa Yogananda Charitable Trust
67	Ananda Image Library
69	Ananda Image Library
72	Ananda Image Library
75	Ananda Image Library
79	Ananda Image Library
80	Nasa.gov, photo by Romeo Durscher
82	"Wavecrest" by Nayaswami Jyotish
85	Photos by Nandini Valeria Cerri
86	Photos by Nandini Valeria Cerri
87	Ananda Image Library
89	"We Are Thine" by Nayaswami Jyotish
90	Photo from pixabay.com
91	Ananda Image Library
92	Paramhansa Yogananda Charitable Trust
93	Paramhansa Yogananda Charitable Trust
96	Ananda Image Library
97	Photo by AnandamayiMa.org
100	Ananda Image Library
102	Ananda Image Library
103	Photo by Nayaswami Devi
106	Ananda Image Library
107	Ananda Image Library
110	Public Domain
111	Ananda Image Library
115	Ananda Image Library
117	Ananda Image Library
120	"Holy Night" by Nayaswami Jyotish
121	Ananda Image Library
124	Photo by Barbara Bingham
126	Photo by NASA
129	Ananda Image Library
131	Photo from LiveinLaughter.com by Premi Grenell
133	Photo from LiveinLaughter.com by Premi Grenell
136	Ananda Image Library
138	Ananda Image Library
139	Photo by Tarini Fisher
140	Photo by NASA.gov

141	Ananda Image Library	197	Photo by Swami Kriyananda
144	Photo from www.AnandamayiMa.org	200	Photo by NASA
147	Photo by Rambhakta	202	Ananda Image Library
148	"Master with the Children" by Nayaswami Jyotish	204	Photo by Kent Williams
		207	Ananda Image Library
151	"First Day of Spring" by Nayaswami Jyotish	210	Ananda Image Library
		211	Ananda Image Library
154	Photo by Nayaswami Jyotish and Devi in Hawaii	212	The Answer Movie
		214	Photo on Facebook Ananda Assisi
156	Photo by National Parks Service	215	Photo on Facebook Ananda Assisi
157	Photo by National Parks Service		
159	Ananda Image Library	218	NASA/JPL-Caltech/SSI/ Hampton University
161	"God's Grace" by Nayaswami Jyotish		
		221	Public Domain
164	Ananda Image Library	224	Ananda Image Library
166	Photo by Nayaswami Jyotish and Devi in India	226	Ananda Image Library
		227	Ananda Image Library
167	Photo by Nayaswami Jyotish and Devi in India	228	Ananda Image Library
		230	Ananda Image Library
168	Photo by Barbara Bingham	232	Ananda Image Library
171	Ananda Image Library	237	Ananda Image Library
173	"To the Mountaintop" by Nayaswami Jyotish	238	Photo by Barbara Bingham
		241	Ananda Image Library
177	Ananda Image Library	245	Ananda Image Library
180	Ananda Image Library	248	Ananda Image Library
181	Photo from pixabay.com	251	Photo by NASA
183	Ananda Image Library	254	Ananda Image Library
186	Photo from pixabay.com	256	"Babaji and Christ" by Nayaswami Jyotish
188	"Devotion" by Nayaswami Jyotish		
191	Photo by Gangamata Glazzard	260	Ananda Image Library
192	Photo by KentWilliamsPhotography.com	262	Ananda Image Library
194	Photo by ShareAlike 2.0		

ABOUT the AUTHORS

Nayaswamis Jyotish and Devi, emissaries of Paramhansa Yogananda, were designated Global Peace Ambassadors by the United Nations. As close friends and students of Swami Kriyananda, Jyotish and Devi have walked the path of meditation, devotion, and service for more than fifty years. Now, as Spiritual Directors of Ananda Worldwide, they travel internationally to share the practical and life-changing teachings of Paramhansa Yogananda and Swami Kriyananda.

Nayaswami Jyotish was named by Swami Kriyananda as his spiritual successor after decades of helping him build Ananda's work around the world. Jyotish began taking classes from Swami Kriyananda in 1967 and together they moved to the rural property in the foothills of the Sierra Nevada Mountains of California in 1969 that is now a model spiritual community, Ananda Village. Jyotish has lectured throughout the world and has helped establish Ananda's work in Italy and India. He has also written several books: *Touch of Light, Touch of Joy, Lessons in Meditation, How* to Meditate, *Thirty-Day Essentials for Marriage*, and *Thirty-Day Essentials for Career.*

Nayaswami Devi first met Swami Kriyananda in 1969 and then and there dedicated her life to the spiritual path. She and Jyotish were married in 1975, and have spent their lives together serving Kriyananda and their guru, Paramhansa Yogananda, through teaching and outreach around the world. Devi is the author of *Touch of Light, Touch of Joy, Faith Is My Armor: The Life of Swami Kriyananda* and the editor of two of Kriyananda's books: *Intuition for Starters* and *The Light of Superconsciousness.*

www.jyotishanddevi.org

More Books by Nayaswamis
JYOTISH AND DEVI

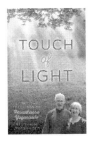

TOUCH OF LIGHT

Living the Teachings of Paramhansa Yogananda
Nayaswamis Jyotish and Devi

Touch of Light is taken from the popular blog entries of the same title. Like the facets of a beautiful diamond, each chapter's topic is a small reflection of the brilliance of one of the great spiritual figures of our time. Paramhansa Yogananda came to the West in 1920, bringing a new vision of how to live. He lectured across the United States drawing thousands, and filling the largest auditoriums. Even after Yogananda's passing in 1952, his *Autobiography of a Yogi* continues to inspire influential people such as George Harrison, Gene Roddenberry (creator of *Star Trek*), and Steve Jobs.

The authors were fortunate to have Kriyananda's training and friendship. They were also founding members of many of these communities. They know from experience that these teachings can improve all aspects of life—health, business, success, creativity, marriage, family, education, and spiritual development.

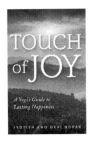

TOUCH OF JOY

A Yogi's Guide to Lasting Happiness
Jyotish and Devi Novak

Joy is an aspect of God, and is at the heart of our own soul nature. It is not to be found in outer fulfillments or gratifications, but exists without any cause. Swami Kriyananda, a direct disciple of Yogananda and spiritual teacher of the authors, once said, "Joy is the solution, not the reward." To learn to live with joy under all circumstances, and not to wait only until conditions are to our liking, is the secret of a happy life.

Jyotish and Devi Novak are celebrated lecturers who have inspired many thousands around the world. They know from experience that these teachings can improve all aspects of life—health, business, success, creativity, marriage, family, education, and spiritual development. The authors, having studied for nearly fifty years with Swami Kriyananda, are Spiritual Directors of Ananda Worldwide and live in Nevada City, California.

FAITH IS MY ARMOR
The Life of Swami Kriyananda
Devi Novak

The life of Swami Kriyananda is the story of a modern-day hero – a man who has achieved extraordinary victories by demonstrating spiritual courage, determination amid great obstacles, and personal sacrifice.

Faith is My Armor tells the complete story of his life: from his childhood in Rumania, to his desperate search for meaning in life, and to his training under his great Guru, the Indian Master, Paramhansa Yogananda. As a youth of 22, he first met and pledged his discipleship to Yogananda, entering the monastery Yogananda had founded in Southern California.

30-DAY ESSENTIALS FOR MARRIAGE
Jyotish Novak

The inspirational ideas in this full color gift book are fun, simple ways to enhance your marriage, helping you improve your life together in just thirty days—one thought for each day of the month. Featuring one inspiring piece of advice and one practical exercise per day, this book is a useful, light-hearted, and eye-catching way for couples—whether engaged, newly married, or together for years—to quickly and gently deepen their relationship.

30-DAY ESSENTIALS FOR CAREER
Jyotish Novak

Whether you are looking for a new job, want to improve your current situation, or simply want to clarify your career goals, *30-Day Essentials for Career* will help. Special emphasis is given to assisting you to develop the attributes and mental skills necessary for breathing new life into your career, by showing you how to become a happier, more effective boss, manager, or employee.

Find, build, and sustain a successful career. These inspirational ideas are simple, effective ways to improve your working life. Discover the essentials of a satisfying career in just thirty days—one thought for each day of the month.

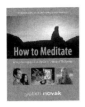

HOW TO MEDITATE

A Step-by-Step Guide to the Art & Science of Meditation
Jyotish Novak

This clear and concise guidebook contains everything you need to start your practice. With easy-to-follow instructions, meditation teacher Jyotish Novak demystifies meditation—presenting the essential techniques so that you can quickly grasp them. *How to Meditate* has helped thousands to establish a regular meditation routine since it was first published in 1989. This newly revised edition includes a bonus chapter on scientific studies showing the benefits of meditation, plus all-new photographs and illustrations.

"The clearest, most practical, and inspiring guide on meditation I've ever read."
— Joseph Bharat Cornell, meditation instructor, author of *Sharing Nature*

"Meditation is a complicated term for something that is truly simple. How To Meditate *is a guide to mastering meditation and reaping more of the benefit of the serenity of the matter. With tips on finding relaxation, opening your natural intuition, and more, this book is a must for those who want to unlock their spirituality."* — Midwest Book Review

LESSONS IN MEDITATION

Jyotish Novak

Small but powerful, this book concisely presents Paramhansa Yogananda's basic spiritual practices, including exercises for relaxation, energization, concentration, meditation, visualization, chanting, and prayer, with simple, "doable" suggestions. These lessons offer the preliminary techniques of Kriya Yoga, including the Hong-Sau concentration technique and Yoganandaji's Energization Exercises for strengthening the body and will power.

FURTHER EXPLORATIONS
WITH CRYSTAL CLARITY

*The original 1946 unedited edition of
Yogananda's spiritual masterpiece*

AUTOBIOGRAPHY OF A YOGI
Paramhansa Yogananda

Autobiography of a Yogi is one of the best-selling Eastern philosophy titles of all time, with millions of copies sold, named one of the best and most influential books of the twentieth century. This highly prized reprinting of the original 1946 edition is the only one available free from textual changes made after Yogananda's death. Yogananda was the first yoga master of India whose mission was to live and teach in the West.

In this updated edition are bonus materials, including a last chapter that Yogananda wrote in 1951, without posthumous changes. This new edition also includes the eulogy that Yogananda wrote for Gandhi, and a new foreword and afterword by Swami Kriyananda, one of Yogananda's close, direct disciples.

This edition of *Autobiography of a Yogi* is also available in unabridged audiobook (MP3) format, read by Swami Kriyananda, Yogananda's direct disciple.

"In the original edition, published during Yogananda's life, one is more in contact with Yogananda himself. While Yogananda founded centers and organizations, his concern was more with guiding individuals to direct communion with Divinity rather than with promoting any one church as opposed to another. This spirit is easier to grasp in the original edition of this great spiritual and yogic classic."
—**David Frawley,** Director, American Institute of Vedic Studies, author of *Yoga and Ayurveda*

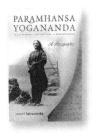

PARAMHANSA YOGANANDA

A Biography with Personal Reflections and Reminiscences
by Swami Kriyananda

Paramhansa Yogananda's classic *Autobiography of a Yogi* is more about the saints Yogananda met than about himself—in spite of the fact that Yogananda was much greater than many he described. Now, one of Yogananda's few remaining direct disciples relates the untold story of this great spiritual master and world teacher: his teenage miracles, his challenges in coming to America, his national lecture campaigns, his struggles to fulfill his world-changing mission amid incomprehension and painful betrayals, and his ultimate triumphant achievement. Kriyananda's subtle grasp of his guru's inner nature reveals Yogananda's many-sided greatness. Includes many never-before-published anecdotes.

"Swami Kriyananda's biography is a welcome addition to the growing literature on Paramhansa Yogananda. I especially like the author's chapter on Yogananda's legacy where he quotes Yogananda on his concept of 'world brotherhood colonies.' I am astounded to find that a consciousness-based theory of evolution predicts the evolutionary necessity of such colonies. Yogananda was a true seer and indeed, his words 'shall not die.'"

—**Amit Goswami,** PhD, quantum physicist and author of *The Self-Aware Universe, Creative Evolution,* and *How Quantum Activism Can Save Civilization*

Also available in unabridged audiobook (MP3) format.

THE NEW PATH

My Life with Paramhansa Yogananda
Swami Kriyananda

Winner of the 2010 Eric Hoffer Award for Best Self-Help/Spiritual Book
Winner of the 2010 USA Book News Award for Best Spiritual Book

This is the moving story of Kriyananda's years with Paramhansa Yogananda, India's emissary to the West and the first yoga master to spend the greater part of his life in America. When Swami Kriyananda discovered *Autobiography of a Yogi* in 1948, he was totally new to Eastern teachings. This is a great advantage to the Western reader, since Kriyananda walks us along the yogic path as he discovers it from the moment of his initiation as a disciple of Yogananda. With winning honesty, humor, and deep insight, he shares his journey on the spiritual path through personal stories and experiences.

Through more than four hundred stories of life with Yogananda, we tune in more deeply to this great master and to the teachings he brought to the West. This book is an ideal complement to *Autobiography of a Yogi*.

"*Reading* Autobiography of a Yogi *by Yogananda was a transformative experience for me and for millions of others. In* The New Path, *Kriyananda carries on this great tradition. Highly recommended."* —**Dean Ornish**, MD, Founder and President, Preventative Medicine Research Institute, Clinical Professor of Medicine, University of California, San Francisco, author of *The Spectrum*

"*Completely revised and updated,* The New Path *is filled with profound reflections, insights, experiences, challenges, and spiritual wisdom. Required reading for every spiritual seeker. I heartily recommend it."* —**Michael Toms**, Founder, New Dimensions Media, and author of *True Work* and *An Open Life: Joseph Campbell in Conversation with Michael Toms*

Also available in unabridged audiobook (MP3) format.

THE ESSENCE OF THE BHAGAVAD GITA

Explained by Paramhansa Yogananda
As Remembered by his disciple, Swami Kriyananda

Rarely in a lifetime does a new spiritual classic appear that has the power to change people's lives and transform future generations. This is such a book.

This revelation of India's best-loved scripture approaches it from a fresh perspective, showing its deep allegorical meaning and its down-to-earth practicality. The themes presented are universal: how to achieve victory in life in union with the divine; how to prepare for life's "final exam," death, and what happens afterward; how to triumph over all pain and suffering.

"*It is doubtful that there has been a more important spiritual writing in the last fifty years than this soul-stirring, monumental work. What a gift! What a treasure!*"
—**Neale Donald Walsch**, author of *Conversations with God*

Also available in unabridged audiobook (MP3) format.

REVELATIONS OF CHRIST

Proclaimed by Paramhansa Yogananda
Presented by his disciple, Swami Kriyananda

The rising tide of alternative beliefs proves that now, more than ever, people are yearning for a clear-minded and uplifting understanding of the life and teachings of Jesus Christ.

This galvanizing book, presenting the teachings of Christ from the experience and perspective of Paramhansa Yogananda, one of the greatest spiritual masters of the twentieth century, finally offers the fresh perspective on Christ's teachings for which the world has been waiting. This work offers us an opportunity to understand and apply the Scriptures in a more reliable way than any other: by studying under those saints who have communed directly, in deep ecstasy, with Christ and God.

"Kriyananda's revelatory book gives us the enlightened, timeless wisdom of Jesus the Christ in a way that addresses the challenges of twenty-first century living." —**Michael Beckwith**, Founder and Spiritual Director, Agape International Spiritual Center, author of *Inspirations of the Heart*

Also available in unabridged audiobook (MP3) format.

CONVERSATIONS WITH YOGANANDA

Recorded, Compiled, and Edited with commentary by his disciple, Swami Kriyananda

Here is an unparalleled, firsthand account of the teachings of Paramhansa Yogananda. Featuring nearly 500 never-before-released stories, sayings, and insights, this is an extensive, yet eminently accessible treasure trove of wisdom from one of the 20th century's most famous yoga masters. Compiled and edited with commentary by Swami Kriyananda, one of Yogananda's closest direct disciples.

THE ESSENCE OF SELF-REALIZATION

The Wisdom of Paramhansa Yogananda
Recorded, Compiled, and Edited by his disciple, Swami Kriyananda

With nearly three hundred sayings rich with spiritual wisdom, this book is the fruit of a labor of love. A glance at the table of contents will convince the reader of the vast scope of this work. It offers as complete an explanation of life's true purpose, and of the way to achieve that purpose, as may be found anywhere.

Also available in unabridged audiobook (MP3) format.

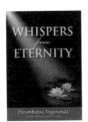

WHISPERS FROM ETERNITY

*Paramhansa Yogananda
Edited by his disciple, Swami Kriyananda*

Many poetic works can inspire, but few, like this one, have the power to change your life. Yogananda was not only a spiritual master, but a master poet, whose verses revealed the hidden divine presence behind even everyday things. This book has the power to rapidly accelerate your spiritual growth, and provides hundreds of delightful ways for you to begin your own conversation with God.

Also available in unabridged audiobook (MP3) format.

~ THE WISDOM OF YOGANANDA SERIES ~

This series features writings of Paramhansa Yogananda not available elsewhere—including many from his earliest years in America—in an approachable, easy-to-read format. The words of the Master are presented with minimal editing, to capture his expansive and compassionate wisdom, his sense of fun, and his practical guidance.

HOW TO BE HAPPY ALL THE TIME
The Wisdom of Yogananda Series, VOLUME 1
Paramhansa Yogananda

Yogananda powerfully explains virtually everything needed to lead a happier, more fulfilling life. Topics include: looking for happiness in the right places; choosing to be happy; tools and techniques for achieving happiness; sharing happiness; balancing success and happiness; and many more.

"*The most important condition for happiness is even-mindedness, and here [Yogananda] brings some of this sense to a treatise on how to be happy under virtually any condition. [This book] is a fine starting point for reaching contentment.*" —**Bookwatch**

KARMA AND REINCARNATION
The Wisdom of Yogananda Series, VOLUME 2
Paramhansa Yogananda

Yogananda reveals the truth behind karma, death, reincarnation, and the afterlife. With clarity and simplicity, he makes the mysterious understandable. Topics include: why we see a world of suffering and inequality; how to handle the challenges in our lives; what happens at death, and after death; and the purpose of reincarnation.

"*Explains more clearly, and from a higher perspective, what happens when we die and afterwards, than any other book I've seen.*"
—**Richard Salva**, author of *The Reincarnation of Abraham Lincoln*

HOW TO BE A SUCCESS
The Wisdom of Yogananda Series, VOLUME 4
Paramhansa Yogananda

This book includes the complete text of *The Attributes of Success*, the original booklet later published as *The Law of Success*. In addition, you will learn how to find your purpose in life, develop habits of success, eradicate habits of failure, develop will power and magnetism, and thrive in the right job.

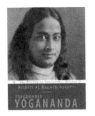

SPIRITUAL RELATIONSHIPS

The Wisdom of Yogananda Series, VOLUME 3
Paramhansa Yogananda

This book contains practical guidance and fresh insight on relationships of all types. Topics include: how to cure bad habits that can end true friendship; how to choose the right partner; sex in marriage and how to conceive a spiritual child; problems that arise in marriage; the Universal Love behind all your relationships.

"*[A] thoroughly 'user friendly' guide on how yoga principles can actually help relationships grow and thrive. Yogananda's keys to understanding yoga's underlying philosophy [teach] how to cure bad habits, expand love's boundaries, and understand relationship problems.*"
—James A. Cox, Chief Editor, *The Bookwatch*

HOW HAVE COURAGE, CALMNESS AND CONFIDENCE

The Wisdom of Yogananda Series, VOLUME 5
Paramhansa Yogananda

Winner of the 2011 International Book Award for Best Self-Help Title

This book shows you how to transform your life. Dislodge negative thoughts and depression. Uproot fear and thoughts of failure. Cure nervousness and systematically eliminate worry from your life. Overcome anger, sorrow, over-sensitivity, and a host of other troublesome emotional responses; and much more.

HOW TO ACHIEVE GLOWING HEALTH AND VITALITY

The Wisdom of Yogananda Series, VOLUME 6
Paramhansa Yogananda

Paramhansa Yogananda offers practical, wide-ranging, and fascinating suggestions on how to have more energy and live a radiantly healthy life. The principles in this book promote physical health and all-round well-being, mental clarity, and ease and inspiration in your spiritual life.

Readers will discover the priceless Energization Exercises for rejuvenating the body and mind, the fine art of conscious relaxation, and helpful diet tips for health and beauty.

~ ~ ~ ~ ~ ~ ~

THE ART AND SCIENCE OF RAJA YOGA

Swami Kriyananda

This book contains fourteen lessons in which the original yoga science emerges in all its glory—a proven system for realizing one's spiritual destiny. This is the most comprehensive course available on yoga and meditation today. Over 450 pages of text and photos give you a complete and detailed presentation of yoga postures, yoga philosophy, affirmations, meditation instruction, and breathing practices.

Also included are suggestions for daily yoga routines, information on proper diet, recipes, and alternative healing techniques.

MEDITATION FOR STARTERS

Swami Kriyananda

Have you wanted to learn to meditate, but just never got around to it? Or tried "sitting in the silence" only to find yourself too restless to stay more than a few moments? If so, *Meditation for Starters* is just what you've been looking for—and with a companion CD, it provides everything you need to begin a meditation practice.

Filled with easy-to-follow instructions, beautiful guided visualizations, and answers to important questions on meditation, the book includes: what meditation is (and isn't); how to relax your body and prepare yourself for going within; and techniques for interiorizing and focusing the mind.

AWAKEN TO SUPERCONSCIOUSNESS

Swami Kriyananda

This popular guide includes everything you need to know about the philosophy and practice of meditation, and how to apply the meditative mind to resolve common daily conflicts in uncommon, superconscious ways.

Superconsciousness is the hidden mechanism at work behind intuition, spiritual and physical healing, successful problem solving, and finding deep and lasting joy.

"A brilliant, thoroughly enjoyable guide to the art and science of meditation. [Swami Kriyananda] entertains, informs, and inspires—his enthusiasm for the subject is contagious. This book is a joy to read from beginning to end." —**Yoga International**

CRYSTAL CLARITY PUBLISHERS

Crystal Clarity Publishers offers many additional resources to assist you in your spiritual journey, including many other books, a wide variety of inspirational and relaxation music composed by Swami Kriyananda, and yoga and meditation videos. To request a catalog, place an order for the above products, or to find out more information, please contact us at:

Crystal Clarity Publishers / www.crystalclarity.com
14618 Tyler Foote Rd. / Nevada City, CA 95959
TOLL FREE: 800.424.1055 or 530.478.7600 / FAX: 530.478.7610
EMAIL: clarity@crystalclarity.com

For our online catalog, complete with secure ordering, please visit our website.

ANANDA WORLDWIDE

Ananda Sangha, a worldwide organization founded by Swami Kriyananda, offers spiritual support and resources based on the teachings of Paramhansa Yogananda. There are Ananda spiritual communities in Nevada City, Sacramento, Palo Alto, and Los Angeles, California; Seattle, Washington; Portland and Laurelwood, Oregon; as well as a retreat center and European community in Assisi, Italy, and communities near New Delhi and Pune, India. Ananda supports more than 140 meditation groups worldwide.

For more information about Ananda Sangha, communities, or meditation groups near you, please call 530.478.7560 or visit www.ananda.org.

THE EXPANDING LIGHT

Ananda's guest retreat, The Expanding Light, offers a varied, year-round schedule of classes and workshops on yoga, meditation, and spiritual practice. You may also come for a relaxed personal renewal, participating in ongoing activities as much or as little as you wish. The beautiful serene mountain setting, supportive staff, and delicious vegetarian food provide an ideal environment for a truly meaningful, spiritual vacation.

For more information, please call 800.346.5350 or visit www.expandinglight.org.